The World of Architecture

ROMANESQUE ARCHITECTURE

Some other books by Bruce Allsopp

A General History of Architecture
A History of Renaissance Architecture
A History of Classical Architecture
Decoration and Furniture
Historic Architecture of Newcastle upon Tyne
Historic Architecture of Northumberland *(In collaboration
    with Ursula Clark)*
The Great Tradition of Western Architecture *(In
    collaboration with H. W. Booton and Ursula Clark)*
Art and the Nature of Architecture
Style in the Visual Arts
The Future of the Arts
The Study of Architectural History
Civilization – the next stage

ORIEL GUIDES
(In collaboration with Ursula Clark)

Architecture of France
Architecture of Italy
Architecture of England

HISTORICAL NOVELS ABOUT MEROVINGIEN FRANCE

Possessed
The Naked Flame
To Kill a King

The World of Architecture
Editor: J. H. Cheetham

ROMANESQUE ARCHITECTURE
The Romanesque Achievement

Bruce Allsopp

THE JOHN DAY COMPANY
New York

The John Day Company, 257 Park Avenue South, New York N.Y. 10010
an Intext publisher

Library of Congress Catalogue Card Number: 76-113423
Printed in Great Britain

ACKNOWLEDGEMENTS

Drawings by Richard Coad
Photographs by the author except:
Ursula Clark, Lessay p. 49, Córdoba p. 52, León p. 53,
Soria p. 55, Brinkburn p. 74, Romsey p. 83
Peter Chatfield, Titchwell p. 87
Aerofilms, Reculver p. 63
Spanish Tourist Office, Orviedo p. 52, Zamora, San Pedro
p. 54
Harold Booton, Zamora p. 54

Contents

Introduction

This book covers a time span of nine hundred years in Western Europe, from the decline of the Roman Empire to the close of the twelfth century. During this period Western civilization almost perished and two great religions came into being. The Mediterranean, which had been the unifying means of communication, became a frontier between Christianity and Islam. Rome ceased to be the administrative centre at the beginning of our period. Constantinople took its place but could not rule the West. Barbarians came in, many of them already half-civilized by Rome but incapable of founding secure communities. Even the Emperor Charlemagne thought of his dominions as personal property to be divided among his heirs according to Frankish usage. Only at the end of the period do we begin to discern acceptance of duties as well as the rights of kingship. Not until the tenth century does civilization begin to reconstitute itself. One puts it in this rather tendentious way because it is not possible to say that men consciously or effectively remade it; indeed, the history of the whole period is fraught with folly, greed and brutality though it is enlightened by faith, heroism and sometimes extreme generosity.

Our purpose here is to see these centuries through the history of their architecture. There are gaps in the evidence and much of the period is deeply obscure. At the end of it an architecture of great beauty arose but it did not happen suddenly. When we look at the forms of Romanesque architecture, in its mature development, in the twelfth century at Pisa, in Burgundy, in Normandy or in England, we find that many of the characteristics of classical architecture have survived the centuries of apparent neglect and decay. What is even more surprising, and heartening to those who believe in the destiny of men, is that the new architecture has new qualities and embodies many improvements upon Roman design.

The Romanesque period was, like our own, a time of change, of reappraisal, of great trouble and adjustment to new conditions. For a long time it was backward-looking. Then, though political and social conditions at the time were appalling, it seems that the tide of human feeling changed. Men began to build again with a new confidence, new ideas, a new vision of what architecture and life were about. Though there are dark passages in the history of the Romanesque—for population declined to perhaps a tenth of what it had been, and many lands were scourged by

7

barbarians who were little better than parasites upon the horses they rode—and though the study of the period in greater depth than is revealed in these pages necessarily harrows the mind, it was one of the most creative periods in human history. This is fully revealed in its architecture.

1 Christian Roman Architecture

Three hundred and thirteen years after the birth of Jesus the Emperor Constantine granted toleration to Christians by the Edict of Milan. Their confiscated properties were to be restored, they could worship in public, they could build churches and their congregations were recognized as corporate bodies which could own property. Though there had been secret churches, some of which survive in the catacombs of Rome and elsewhere, this was the real beginning of Christian architecture in the Roman Empire. This was the soil out of which Romanesque architecture was to grow.

Romanesque is the name we give to Christian architecture in Western Europe from the end of the Roman Empire to about the close of the twelfth century. It is the architecture of a long period of struggle, suffering and invention leading to two centuries of glorious achievement. It can be specially interesting to us, in the twentieth century, because it was a new and experimental architecture, evolved in a restless and anxious age during which there were fundamental changes in the ways men lived and thought.

Having recognized Christianity, the Emperor Constantine took another decision of outstanding historical importance, and moved the capital of the Empire to Byzantium, a predominantly Greek city renamed after him, Constantinople. The new capital was situated at the most important convergence of land and sea routes in the Empire while Rome itself, no longer the centre of administration, and inconveniently located halfway down the limb of Italy, declined in population, wealth and influence. The architectural forms which Roman architects had created from a fusion of Greek and Etruscan design, as symbolic of Roman citizenship from Spain to Syria and from Britain to the Sahara desert, no longer had the validity of reference to the capital and all that Rome had stood for in culture, government and pagan religion.

In the new Christian capital, Constantinople, Greek architects quickly invented new ways of building in which the dome supported on pendentives was a predominant structural feature. By the time of the Emperor Justinian, in the sixth century, the Church of the Holy Wisdom (Sancta Sophia) had crowned their achievement, which was to affect all Christian architecture of the Eastern Empire and become characteristic of the Orthodox Church up to the present day. When, in the seventh century, the Islamic religion inspired Arab conquests of many lands which had been part

9

of the Roman Empire, the Arabs learned from Byzantine architects and made their manner of design the characteristic architecture of Islam. To the twin branches, Christian and Islamic, which came from the inventions of Hellenic architects in the Eastern Empire during the fourth to sixth centuries, the name *Hellenesque* is given. This recognizes its Greek origin and distinguishes it from the Romanesque architecture of the West, which developed differently and much more slowly.

It is not possible to draw a line across the map of Europe and say that Hellenesque lies to the east and Romanesque to the west of it. The division is blurred. Generally however it is true to say that the principal territory of Romanesque architecture is Italy, France, the Low Countries, Western Germany and Switzerland, Britain and parts of Spain. It should also be remembered that during the whole of the period other countries, both Christian and Islamic, were more prosperous, populous and civilized than Western Europe. It is not surprising, therefore, that Hellenesque architecture influenced the development of Romanesque at many times and places.

In the fourth and fifth centuries Roman civilization declined in the West. But the process was slow and the eclipse of Rome seems to have favoured the development of other cities, in Northern Italy, France and Germany, as regional centres. Among these one of the most interesting is Trier, where two great thermal establishments, a palace and a vast double cathedral were built. Because Trier has never since achieved any comparable importance as a city, rather more survives there than at Milan, Cologne, Clermont or Paris.

In the West, architects continued to design in the traditional Roman way and we can see this at Trier, but what concerns us in this volume are those aspects of late Roman architecture which were to lead to Roman-

esque ways of building and in particular to the design of churches, the principal achievement of Romanesque architects. Essentially, Romanesque architecture was the architecture of emergent Christendom in the West.

The Roman temple was not suitable for Christian worship and as their power grew, Christian congregations quickly eliminated pagan establishments. There are accounts of zealous expeditions to destroy the sanctuaries of Roman gods, such as the temples of Mercury on the tops of the Puy-de-Dôme and Montmartre in Paris. Pagan statues were smashed or drowned in lakes and rivers, but the finely wrought columns of temples were often taken away to be re-used in building Christian Churches.

The origin of the Christian church plan has been much disputed. One view, expressed by Sir Alfred Clapham, is that it was simply designed to satisfy the needs of the ritual. On the other hand, architects of the period were bound to have been influenced by the plan forms then common, so one should consider these. One form was the Roman town house in

Plan of a Roman House with atrium and main room

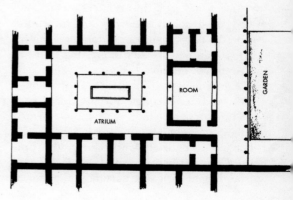

which there had been secret meetings for worship under the persecution.

Another probable influence upon the church plan was the kind of building readily available to Christians when they were free to worship in public. They could then purchase, or hire, public or private halls of the kind which Romans had evolved for courts of justice and public meetings. These buildings were called *basilicas* and were of two main structural types. Some of the more monumental basilicas were vaulted but most were roofed with pitched timber roofs. Often there was an apse at the far end where the rostrum had been and in this apse it was natural to place the table or altar. Palace halls, which were used in the time of Constantine, were also of this form. Constantine's own church in Rome was basilican. (The arguments are well set out by Michael Gough in *The Early Christians*, London 1961.)

Some churches used another and quite different type of plan common in Roman cities. This was circular and employed the structural device of a dome to cover it. Often the circular space was surrounded by a colonnade. Such a building was particularly suitable for the service of baptism and, later, it became common in Italy to build such circular baptisteries adjoining large churches of basilican plan, as at Pisa and Florence.

The structural forms available to Christian architects of the declining Western Empire were all those which Rome had used in the days of its greatness, but economic considerations generally ruled out the massive structures which were necessary to support Roman vaulting. In fact, as the section (p. 12) shows, the typical Christian basilica was remarkably frail and economical in structure. It was virtually four parallel walls spanned by light timber roof trusses.

In decoration the Christians continued to use Roman patterns in marble and mosaic, but Constantinople set the fashions in decorative design. In particular, its taste for large surfaces covered with pictorial mosaics was influential. Byzantine decorative motifs affected alike architecture, manuscripts and vestments. Designs which in the East would have been executed in mosaics of marble and glass

Plan of a centralized church with narthex

Plan of a vaulted basilica

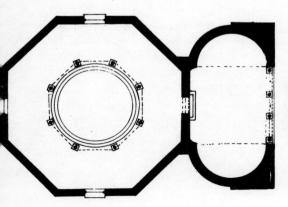

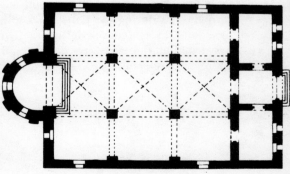

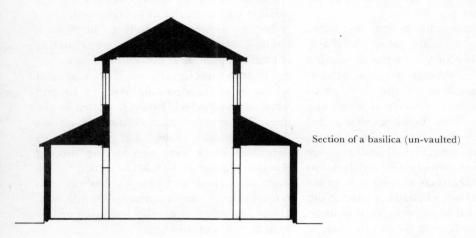

Section of a basilica (un-vaulted)

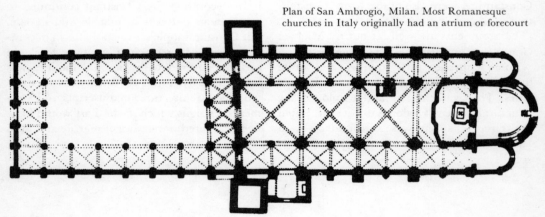

Plan of San Ambrogio, Milan. Most Romanesque
churches in Italy originally had an atrium or forecourt

were often done with painted plaster in the impoverished West.

Much fine work was carried out in the Western Empire during the fourth and fifth centuries, and the evidence of decline is often exaggerated. But the end was coming, and though many large churches are recorded as having been built there was no sign that a new and splendid architecture would emerge in the West. Before that could happen Western civilization was to be brought to the brink of extinction, partly by invasions but more by fratricidal warfare, incompetent government and widespread disease.

2 Romanesque in Italy

The adoption of Christianity by the Roman government did little or nothing to humanise its harsh administration or ameliorate the growing social distress in Italy during the fourth century. At the beginning of the fifth century the Goths began to move in. The first wave of Ostrogoths reached Fiesole, north of Florence, and were defeated there in 406. In 410, Alaric the Visigoth, in a lightning campaign, sacked Rome itself and reached Reggio, where he died. Another wave of Ostrogoths won a decisive victory on the River Adda, near Milan, in 490 and in 493 Theodoric, their king, made himself ruler of Italy with his headquarters at Ravenna, having spent ten years as a hostage at the Roman court in Constantinople. In 536 a Roman army entered Italy from Sicily and for eighteen years Justinian's generals conducted a savage war of reconquest during which a third of the population perished. A Byzantine *exarch* (i.e. viceroy) was established at Ravenna and some splendid buildings were erected, probably by architects from Constantinople. One of these, San Vitale, is a characteristic Hellenesque building with a central dome but the other two great churches, Sant' Apollinare Nuovo in Ravenna and Sant' Apollinare at Classe, the now silted-up port of imperial Ravenna, are simple basilicas.

The Roman-Byzantine government in Ravenna had been established by force and it called upon the barbarian Lombards to augment that force. These barbarians soon found that they could take for themselves the power which they had been hired to protect and from the end of the sixth century Lombard kings and dukes dominated most of Italy. Churchmen looked to the Emperor for protection against them. Generally they did not find it.

In the social structure of Italy two main forces emerged. One was the aristocracy, a landowning class of titled nobility, mostly of barbarian origin. They were generally autocratic, quarrelsome, perfidious and irresponsible. On the other side was the Church, whose clergy maintained much closer contact with the people and were to some extent democratically elected.

As early as the end of the fourth century Prudentius had written "All men now live as citizens of the same city or relatives in the same house. . . . The blood of all races mingles, and of many nations is formed one people." He saw heaven itself as "celestial Rome". On this idealized basis Rome became the religious capital of the Romanesque western world and the seat of the Popes of the Catholic Church. Throughout Western Europe (and this is a remarkable feature of the period) warring armies often respected the properties of the Church, which became sanctuaries in a very practical sense. Furthermore, even the brief recital of the history of Italy given here indicates a massive load of human suffering; the new religion extended towards the miseries of humanity in a violent world the compassion of Christ.

Wealthy men built for security on the crags of mountains and the ruins of their rugged towers still punctuate the Italian landscape. In the cities and villages men devoted what might seem, in another and less devout age, a disproportionate amount of their small wealth to building churches. One could believe that these, at least, would endure in a chaotic world. Endure they did. A surprising number of the fine churches in Italy visited by modern tourists owe their origin, and even substantial parts of their structure, to Christians of the sixth and seventh centuries. A splendid and readily accessible example is Santa Maria in Trastevere in Rome, but, as in most other cases, what we now see was mostly rebuilt in the early twelfth century. The Italians are an industrious people with a strong taste for alteration and embellishment. Enthusiasm for antiquity often leads to the ascription of very early dates to Romanesque churches in guide books and elsewhere. Most of these are, to say the least, dubious. Some of the doubt arises from the fact that from the sixth to the eleventh century in Italy, poverty and anarchy prevailed and there was little development in architecture. Thus the Church of San Clemente in Rome, originally built in the fourth century, is cited in many books as being of that date. Yet modern research has established that what we see now was rebuilt, after partial destruction in the fire of 1084, and incorporated a chancel built in 872. The rebuilding was completed about 1130.

A great early church which survived all the disasters in the medieval history of Rome was old St Peter's but it was pulled down during the Renaissance in order to make way for the present cathedral. One can get a good idea of what was sacrificed by visiting the restored church of St Paul outside the Walls. This is a truly magnificent basilican church of great dignity and simplicity, and perhaps the finest monument there is to the vigour of Christian architecture in its earliest days.

Existing buildings and fragments afford a tantalising glimpse of early Christian architecture. Patient scholarship is gradually extending knowledge, but it would be foolish to pretend that we know very much about early Romanesque architecture in Italy. This being so, any generalizations must be attempted and accepted with extreme caution and students of the subject must expect to proceed with the patient techniques of the archaeologist. In considering the history of European Romanesque architecture as a whole, it is well to recognise obscurity, where it does exist, as a challenge to the curiosity of the serious scholar. We must not pretend that what is obscure can be made clear in a few facile sentences.

The history of early Italian Romanesque architecture is further complicated by legends which have received more academic support than they deserve. In particular, the subject is confused by the advent of the Lombards who overwhelmed the Byzantine rulers of Ravenna in 752. Dr K.J. Conant has stated the problem admirably: "With regard to the Lombards a difficulty arises from the fact that their name has been given to the great region of north Italy (although it was in anarchy while they attempted to rule it), and also to a great style of architecture (although they were destroyers rather than builders)."

Among the reasons for identifying a "Lombardic style" of architecture has been the reluctance of Christian historians to recognise the extent of Islamic influence upon Italian architecture. The visitor to southern Italy should be warned that in guide books, and elsewhere, the term "Lombardic" is not uncommonly a Christian euphemism for "Saracenic".

Nonetheless, it was in what we now call Lombardy (though not because of the Lombards) that one of the earliest coherent systems of Romanesque architecture emerged. Milan is a naturally rich city commanding the inexhaustibly fertile valley of the Po. It had been the centre of administration for Italy under the emperor Diocletian and its great bishop, Saint Ambrose, baptized Saint Augustine there in 384. Though the administration moved to Ravenna in 402, Milan remained prosperous, even under Lombard misrule. When that was terminated, the new architecture developed between the poles of Milan and Ravenna, deriving strength through the one from France and through the other from Constantinople.

By the middle of the seventh century, in this region, there was a pattern of building organization which was to persist throughout the Middle Ages and profoundly influence the character of medieval architecture. As early as 642 a charter refers to *magistri commacini* or *comacini*. Though the suggestion has been made (and greatly elaborated) that these were members of a guild based upon the city of Como it seems much more likely that they were a guild of masons who worked together. The etymology of the word *mason* is intriguingly dubious, but *macina* can mean scaffold and *comacini* may thus be *companions of the scaffold*. Whatever the derivation, the existence of a group, or guild, of masons who developed common trade techniques and practices seems certain. The designer-architect of these days seems to have been, as he remained until the Renaissance, a master mason, a *mechanikos* in Greek, and the word *architecton* was applied to the master of the works, or clerk of the works as he came to be known in medieval England.

The great achievement of the masons of Lombardy was to lay the technical foundations upon which a great style of design could develop. This they did mainly by improving the Roman way of building brick walls. The wall became a more refined structural element and much of Romanesque architecture, throughout Europe, is "wall architecture". On the surface of the wall, in accordance with human practice from time immemorial, the designers imprinted the earlier architectural style of Rome with pilaster strips surmounted by arches. We still simulate the old in the new, as for example when we make

Amalfi, Arab influence in the cloister

Verona, San Lorenzo. Slender brick walls and groined vaults to aisles and triforium. Re-used Roman columns

Tarquinia, Santa Maria in Castello

electric fires look like log fires, put bonnets and radiator grilles on the fronts of rear-engined automobiles, half-timber on houses and make plastic laminates look like polished walnut. Because the pilaster strips and arcades were there to comply with tradition and make modern architecture easier to the eye, they were no longer controlled by structural necessity. Consequently these pilasters could be played with and elongated at will.

Medieval Italy became a land of small counties and developed into a country of city states when commerce and industry became more influential than the tenure of land. Within these politically and geographically isolated but contentious states individual genius, local pride and the accidents of ethnic and cultural inheritance led to the creation of many local styles. Like the architecture of the Roman Empire, but on a minuscule scale, these styles stood for the patriotic self-consciousness of the city or county. Sometimes, in a society where marriage was an instrument of dynastic alliance and treaties of defence and aggression were com-

mon, curious cross-fertilisations occurred.

Apart from Lombardy and Ravenna, the main areas of Romanesque architecture are Rome itself, Pisa, Florence and the south-east of Italy, which was conquered by the Normans. In each of these areas it is possible to observe influences from outside, not least from Islamic architecture, which was established in Sicily and southern Italy prior to the Norman conquest.

As one might expect, the Roman tradition remained strongest in Rome itself, which gradually rose again to prosperity and importance as the seat of the Popes. Characteristic Roman churches of the Romanesque period are basilican with a narthex and atrium (usually now destroyed) and colonnades or arcades of plundered or imitated classical columns. Many of these were much altered in the seventeenth and eighteenth centuries by Baroque schemes of decoration which, in some cases, gave them a flavour more Roman than Romanesque. Twenty miles away from Rome, at Tarquinia, the splendid but neglected church of Santa Maria in

Rome, Santa Maria in Trastevere: a typical basilican church probably dating from the seventh century but largely rebuilt in the twelfth century and embellished later

Benevento, Santa Sophia, the cloister (now part of the museum)

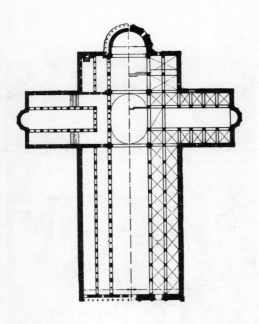

Plan of Pisa Cathedral

Castello has affinities with both Norman and Pisan architecture, from roughly equidistant centres of influence, north and south along the coast.

The Pisan style of design was established in the same creative period which saw the conquest of Sicily by the Normans. The cathedral, which was to be part of one of the greatest architectural achievements in the world, was begun in 1063. The original architect was Buschetus. The western extension of the nave was designed by Rainaldus and completed in 1272. In plan this remarkable church consists simply of three basilicas, one being the main body and the other two forming the transepts. The crossing is rectangular in plan and surmounted by an elliptical dome. The exterior is covered with arcading in fine marble, designed and carved with a sensitivity and precision which excels much genuine Roman work and merits comparison with Hellenistic buildings such as the Tower of the Winds at Athens. Naturally enough the

Pisan achievement was influential elsewhere, and particularly at Lucca and as far away as Arezzo. Architectonically the building is remarkably clean and simple. Every functional and structural element is clearly articulated. Upon these pure forms a rigorously consistent decorative pattern of arcading is imposed.

Stylistically the group at Pisa is interesting in that it is consistent over a building period of two centuries. The belfry (the famous "Leaning Tower") begun in 1271 by Gerardo and completed c.1350, matches the arcading of the cathedral, thus confuting the common belief that medieval architects always designed in the modern style of the day. The Baptistery, designed by Diotisalvi, was begun in 1153 and is notable for its perfection of detailing, as well as for its conical roof, which may have been derived from Palestine whither Pisan ships were conveying crusaders and pilgrims at the time of its building. This cone was partly masked by a Gothic-style dome, 1250–65.

Architecture does not begin and end with single buildings and at Pisa we have one of the supreme examples of the successful relationship of buildings to form a group and create an environment.

In Florence, San Miniato al Monte, of which the interior was completed in 1062, is a classical basilica with very pure detailing. It may indeed have been regarded as a genuine Roman building by the great Renaissance architect Brunelleschi and so have influenced his design for the loggia of the 'Spedale degli Innocenti. But the outstanding Romanesque building of the city which gave birth to Renaissance architecture is the Baptistery of San Giovanni. It is octagonal and has a dome spanning ninety feet. The date is uncertain but the foundations are probably fifth century, all above them belonging to the eleventh and twelfth centuries with later embellishments. It is interesting to compare its elegant and economical structure with the massive walls and dome of the Pantheon in Rome in order to realise the improvement in structural technique which had been wrought by Romanesque builders during the so-called Dark Ages.

In southern Italy the Normans built a group of churches along the Apulian coast. These have something in common with early Norman architecture in France but influences came from Lombardy also. It is interesting to compare San Nicola at Bari with San Zeno Maggiore at Verona. Among other similarities both have a western portal with columns carried on the backs of animals. This motif became common in the eleventh and twelfth centuries and may have been invented by Guglielmus, one of the first great sculptors of the Italian Romanesque, who is known to have made the Bari throne in San Nicola in 1098.

There is a beautiful and ornate church at Manfredonia and then, farther north, at Ancona we find a meeting of many influences, a kind of summation of Italian Romanesque

Bari, San Nicola, interior

Pisa Cathedral, the east end

Pisa Baptistry, interior looking up into the conical dome

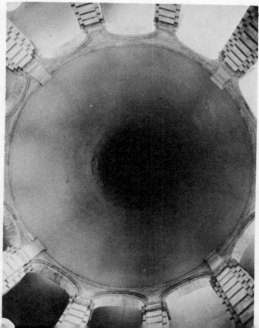

Verona, San Zeno Maggiore, interior

in the cathedral and in the church of Santa Maria at Portonuovo.

For the summit of Italian achievement in the Romanesque period we must return to the north. The great domed cathedrals of St Mark at Venice and St Anthony at Padua belong predominantly to the Hellenesque tradition; but from Verona to Milan and Pavia and up into the valleys, to Aosta and Susa (both places with important Roman remains even to the present day) Romanesque architecture flourished. In the rich cities of Milan and Pavia we discover a new aspect of Italian Romanesque architecture, for here there is structural inventiveness and an interest in the problems of vaulting which we do not find in more southern parts. The church of San Ambrogio in Milan, one of the very few that retains its atrium complete (see p. 12), is a complex and adventurous structure with two bays of aisle to one bay of nave. The high vaults of the nave are "domed-up", that is to say, the crown of the vault is higher than the sides and the faces of the vault are domical

Verona, San Zeno Maggiore, detail of bronze doors
(eleventh to twelfth century)

segments. Furthermore, the vaults are ribbed and this was a very important discovery indeed because it heralded the separation of rib and panel, which is one of the inventions that made Gothic architecture possible. The vaults may have been designed as early as 1080 but were probably not built until 1117. There is no certainty in this matter except that San Ambrogio was an adventurous and important structure. Perhaps even more important, it is also a very beautiful church.

On the whole, Italian Romanesque shows much more interest in form and elegance of design, in the creation of calm and spacious interiors without structural fuss, than in technical adventure. It is significant that structural experiment is largely limited to the northwest where the mountain passes out of France debouch into the plain of Lombardy.

3 Romanesque in France

Gaul, like Italy, was infiltrated and invaded by barbarian tribes, Visigoths, Burgundians and Franks being the most important. The Burgundians had been granted territories in Savoy by the Roman authorities and moved up into the Rhone valley to establish a capital at Lyons. The Visigoths went into the south-west, had their capital at Toulouse and established themselves in most of Spain. The Franks came into north-eastern Gaul and acquired most of what is now France, Belgium and Germany west of the Rhine. Most barbarians were Arian Christians before they came, but the Franks were still pagan. Their king, Clovis I, accepted Roman Christianity and was baptized at Reims, by St Remy, in 496. This very significant event gave him the support of the Roman clergy in Gaul and resulted in a powerful alliance between Roman Church and Frankish State.

After a reign of fifty years of consolidating Frankish rule the death of the ferocious king Lothar I in 561 apparently came as a great surprise to him, for he exclaimed on his death-bed that he would not believe God could let so great a monarch die! The sharing of his king-dom among four sons led to a long and disastrous civil war. Freak storms, excessively warm winters and terrible summer floods added to the general distress. Though there was a revival of civilized life during the reign of "Good King Dagobert," who ruled from 628 to 638, the Merovingian dynasty of these first Frankish kings declined and effective rule then passed into the hands of the mayors of the palace.

While the sons of Lothar were fighting each other the Lombards had come like birds of prey into Italy, where they established the duchies of Spoleto and Benevento from which they harassed the people and sorely plagued the Church. The Pope appealed to Charles Martel, mayor of the palace and now virtual ruler of the Franks, who had already achieved a remarkable victory for Christendom by defeating the Saracens at Poitiers in 732. But Charles Martel died and his son Pepin the Short answered the call. In return the Pope formally ended the Merovingian line of kings by deposing Childeric and appointing Pepin in his place, thus giving to the Frankish kingship a hitherto undreamed-of sanctity and creating a tremendous precedent.

On Pepin's death the Lombards took up arms and again the Franks came to the rescue, led now by Charlemagne, who took for him-self the Lombard crown and added northern Italy to the Frankish empire. For the last

Above Tours, St Martin in 470 (after K. J. Conant Elements are certain, details hypothetical)

Below Poitiers, the Merovingian Church of St Jean, still in the Roman tradition

quarter of the eighth century Italy was at peace and intrigue flourished. The Papacy assumed supremacy over the whole of the Western Empire and on Christmas Day of the year 800, Charlemagne was crowned Emperor. The Holy Roman Empire, thus created, lasted until 1806. As James Bryce said, "Nothing else so directly linked the old world to the new" though it was "no more than a tradition, a fancied revival of departed glories ... exercising over the minds of men an influence such as its material strength could

above Lorsch (Germany), monastery gateway, *c.*800
below Germigny des Près, exterior

never have commanded."

France, having saved western Christendom from the Saracens in the west and from the Lombards and Greeks in the south, became the principal support of the Papacy, and in return their king was consecrated ruler of the West. France thereby assumed a position of influence in the arts which, consolidated under Louis XIV in the seventeenth century, it has never completely lost. The Church was administered from Rome but, throughout the medieval period, the arts which served it

25

were propagated north of the Alps, until the remarkable phenomenon of the Renaissance, when all this great achievement of Romanesque and Gothic architecture was seen as a barbaric aberration, and Italy reasserted the architectural forms of ancient Rome.

Charlemagne inherited a sad and impoverished kingdom, menaced in the southwest by the Saracens, fighting against whom his paladins Roland and Oliver created a legend. The horrid Lombards were in Italy and the most splendid city in the world was still Constantinople, incomparably greater and more cultured than anything in the West but opposed to the artistic imagery beloved in the West, and particularly to the use of sculpture which was to become the special glory of French Romanesque architecture. Charlemagne began to rebuild after centuries of decay. As might be expected, this "Carolingian" architecture was in the Roman tradition but there were influences from Constantinople, and possibly from Islamic Spain (where Córdoba had risen to be perhaps the second city in the Western world). But one detects a new spirit of hope and adventure in the originality and charm of Carolingian design. Yet it was like a sunrise blotted out by storm clouds and the full glory of the revival of architecture was not to come until the end of the millennium.

The best known of Charlemagne's buildings is the Palatine Chapel, or Minster, at Aachen. It was designed by Odo of Metz and begun in 792. Though restored in 983 and 1881 with some alterations, it survives in substantially its original form, together with vestiges of the palace. Superficially the plan suggests that it is an imitation of San Vitale at Ravenna but in fact, as Conant has pointed out, the structure is essentially Roman, not Byzantine. One may suspect, however, that Charlemagne intended it to compare with the splendid buildings of the East, and it was richly decora-

ted. A chapel at Germigny-des-Près was built in 806 and survived until 1867 when it was ravaged by "a brutal and ignorant restoration." It also has a centralized plan which is probably of Eastern origin.

Louis the Pious succeeded Charlemagne but when he died his sons, like the sons of Lothar, demanding the division of their father's kingdom according to the fatal Frankish custom, went to war with each other. By the partition of Verdun in 843 the Empire was divided into three. Lothar, the eldest son, ruled an impossible strip of territory in the middle, designed to include the two capitals, Aachen and Rome. By 888 the Carolingian Empire had collapsed and Western Europe sank to the lowest depth of disorder and despair. The Saracens dominated the Mediterranean and sacked Rome. The Danes and Norsemen sailed up the rivers of France and Germany slaying, burning and enslaving. The wild Hungarians "carried the terror of their battleaxes to the Apennines and the ocean". It is to this period of chaos that we owe the loss of so much early Romanesque architecture.

In 911 the foundations were laid for the great duchy of Normandy: a new era began and France started to rebuild. The French were virtually a new people synthesized from Celts, Romans, Franks, Burgundians, Normans and others who had wandered or been driven into the former province of Gaul. As might be expected, in a country so formed, with different ethnic groups ascendant in different regions, varied schools of design emerged. One thing they had in common was the genius which had peeped out for a brief time around the end of the eighth century. It was made manifest in structural ingenuity allied to extreme originality in the exploration of architectonic form. There has never been an age which was so inventive in the art of enclosing space by building. Out of the

Germigny-des-Près, interior

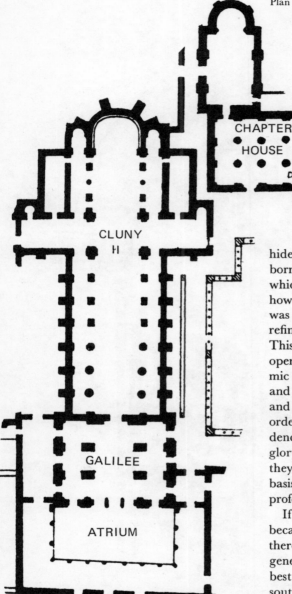

CHAPTER
HOUSE

D O

CLUNY
II

GALILEE

ATRIUM

hideous memory of the ninth century was born, it seems, a resolve to build churches which would not burn. We have already seen how a new and improved wall architecture was developed in the Po valley. Upon this refined structure stone roofs had to be placed. This was the structural challenge which opened architecture to invention. The economic means were provided by the rise in power and influence of the Roman Catholic Church and especially by the growth of the monastic orders. In an age of renewed faith and confidence men built for permanence, for the glory of God, and within reasonable limits they did not count the cost. Here was the basis for a great style of architecture, namely a profound belief in its value.

If we think of Paris as the face of France, because its eyes, ears and mouth seem to be there, Burgundy may well be its heart. This generous region, which produces some of the best wines in the world, is caressed on the south by the River Loire. The Seine rises there and the Saône flows through it to join the Rhône at Lyons. From the Mediterranean, from Italy through the Alpine passes, from Germany and Austria and the East, from the Moselle valley, the Rhineland and the North

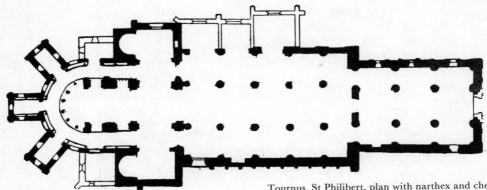

Tournus, St Philibert, plan with narthex and chevet

Sea, all roads lead to Burgundy and in study-ing the history of French Romanesque archi-tecture this is where we should start. The abbey of Cluny, which at its zenith controlled fourteen hundred and fifty religious houses, was sold for demolition after the French Revolution. What little remains is now the principal tourist attraction of a seedy little town which might well have become one of the outstanding resorts of Europe. The extent of its influence upon architectural design is disputed. Cluny was certainly an important centre, but, like many large organizations, possibly somewhat conservative.

The town of Tournus stands at an important crossing of the Saône a few miles north-east of Cluny. To this place a party of monks had brought the relics of Saint Philibert in 875. Their abbey was ravaged by Hungarians in 937 and about 950 they began the church which still stands as one of the most exciting Romanesque designs in France. Originally it was timber roofed, but vaults were added in the eleventh century and completed about 1120. Over the nave, clerestory lighting was ingeniously provided by transverse barrel vaults carried upon diaphragm arches. This church is light and spacious like an Italian basilica but it has the structural tensions which were to characterize French architec-ture for five centuries.

In Tournus we find the typical elements of large French Romanesque churches. There is a spacious narthex, with western towers, occupying the full width of the nave and its aisles. The nave leads to a crossing with north and south transepts projecting beyond the aisles. The crossing is surmounted by a tall square tower. The sanctuary ends in an apse and the aisles go round the apse to form an ambulatory. Three chapels radiate from the ambulatory to form what is called a *chevet,* one of the principal inventions of French medieval architecture.

This plan form, which persisted throughout the Romanesque and Gothic periods, was not only liturgically convenient in providing a number of separate chapels but was also a logical structural system which reached its ultimate development in the Gothic cathedral of Beauvais.

To understand the development of the French cathedral plan we must go back to the basilica, exemplified in its simplest form at Le Thor in Provence, where there is a plain, buttressed hall with an apse at the end. Such a plan could be developed by building tran-septs to make it cruciform, as at Souillac, and additional chapels could be added but they merely opened off the main body of the church and lacked seclusion. The fully developed basilican plan is seen at Autun, where the

29

Tournus, St Philibert, the nave vaults

aisles terminate in apses at the east end, and in this case extra aisles are added to the nave. The chevet was born with the idea of taking the aisles round the main apse – a basically very simple device – but it had the great advantage of providing a buttressing structure for the eastern apse. The radiating chapels then provided further support for the ambulatory, and this was a great advantage because it strengthened the whole east end of the church against the thrust of the tower over the crossing. In fact the tower formed the apex of a pyramid of supporting structure which, of course, extended westwards outside the pyramid to provide the nave of the church.

Internally the chevet provided a sanctuary defined by a curved colonnade beyond which was the spatial depth of the ambulatory and chapels. It was a very powerful architectural form and the French never seem to have tired of it. It even recurs in the chapel J.H.

Tournus, St Philibert, the structural form

Le Thor, a typical Provençal church

Mansart built for Louis XIV at Versailles!

The structural security of the eastern apse had its counterpart at the west end where the high vaults of the nave terminated. The low narthex which had been sufficient for the support of a timber-roofed nave was replaced by squat towers at the end of each aisle. These buttressed the tendency of the end piers of the nave to fall outwards, and from being primarily a structural device they quickly developed into the characteristic west front of a great French church. Any increase in the height of the towers added to their weight and so to their effectiveness in diverting the thrust downwards. In principle this is the same as the pinnacle which loads a flying buttress and diverts the thrust of it downwards, the resultant of two forces acting together being a function of their weight and direction.

South-west of Burgundy lies the beautiful land of Auvergne comprising the fertile valley of the Allier, the vine-growing foothills and the conical volcanic mountains of Puy-de-Dôme. Clermont, its capital, had been an important Roman city but in the troubled sixth century practically the whole region was depopulated by plague, and Gregory of Tours records that a defeated tribe of Saxons were settled there "so that the soil might be cultivated again".

Around Clermont, in the eleventh and twelfth centuries, a remarkable group of

31

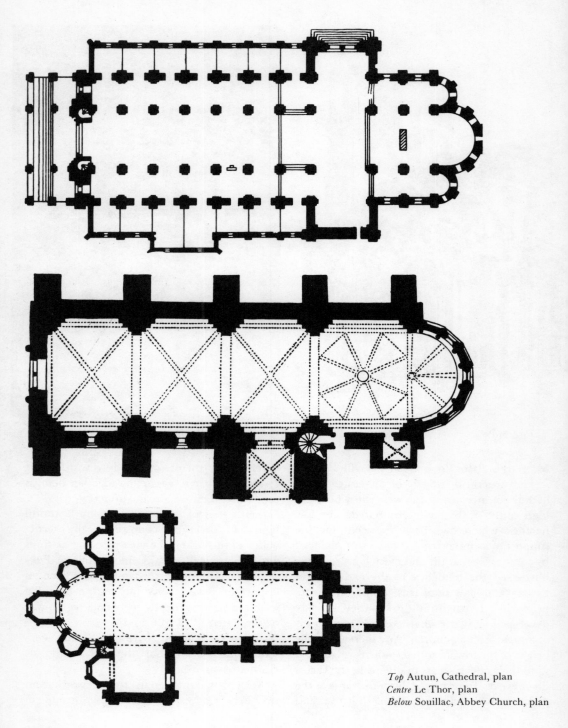

Top Autun, Cathedral, plan
Centre Le Thor, plan
Below Souillac, Abbey Church, plan

32

Autun, Cathedral, interior at the crossing

churches was built. Probably the most important was the second cathedral of Clermont but this was replaced by a Gothic building and the church of Nôtre Dame du Port is usually cited as typical of Auvergne, possibly because it is most accessible, though it is architecturally less satisfying than some of the others and very cluttered with later "embellishments". St Austremoine at Issoire is the most splendid, and Orcival, in a secluded valley beside a trout stream which runs through the village, is perhaps the most beautiful. The Auvergne churches are built of dark igneous stone and have a severe,

Orcival, the crossing from the chevet

and seen in section they appear as rudimentary flying buttresses, but clearly the idea was to get this high light-source at the crossing. An interesting feature is that the main vaults are supported by half-barrel vaults over the triforium again creating the flying buttress effect. The whole roof is solid stone, integral with the vaults and stepped on the outside. Light comes into the nave from windows in the outside wall of the triforium – another striking effect of illumination which seems to have been one of the preoccupations of the Auvergnat architects.

In section, the Auvergne churches are curiously like Greek temples with their naves and aisles covered by a single roof which, if it were projected to the west end of the church instead of being masked by western towers, would appear as a pediment or low-pitched gable. Though the internal mystery of light filtering through the triforium is interesting, this way of design was, in a sense, a backward step, since it rejected the achievement of the Roman basilican design with its great advantage of clerestory lighting to the nave. The problem was, of course, to support a very heavy barrel vault, but why, one may ask, should they use a barrel vault in the early twelfth century? The evidence for an answer to this question can only be circumstantial but, as an eminent judge who is also an architectural historian has pertinently observed, men have been frequently convicted in the courts on circumstantial evidence which may well be more valid than documents which are open to suspicion of inaccuracy, falsification or wishful thinking. So, in considering the nature of the Romanesque achievement, we should not neglect circumstantial evidence as to the motivation of the architects. There are two indications: one is the actual structure and the other is the way architects of later times, including our own, are known to have thought and designed.

chunky character. Inside, the long barrel vaults of the naves are dark and the interiors sombre but magically beautified by the architectonic invention which is characteristic of the whole group, the shouldered or, as some call it, lantern tower. Conant suggests a Carolingian origin for this, but whatever its provenance it is certainly a marvellous design and one especially suitable for the dark stone churches of Auvergne because it pierces the crossing with shafts of light, creating a moving and theatrical effect. The design is best understood from the illustrations. The shoulders which support the octagonal lantern are, in effect, an elevation of the aisle at the crossing,

Ancona, interior (*overleaf*) and exterior of S.M. di
Portonuovo, a perfect example of Romanesque.
Notice the separate expression of each element of
the design

35

Clermont, Nôtre Dame du Port, chevet and tower

The structure of stone-vaulted, fireproof churches evolved from a basilican form of church which was timber-roofed. Such timber roofs would usually be lined by a flat or coffered ceiling. Thus two elements of design were imprinted upon the minds of architects, namely a continuous ceiling giving a long horizontal plane towards the east end and the altar, all supported by timber roof trusses bringing down their loads at intervals along the walls. Instead of trusses there might be in some churches trussed rafters, which when lined with timber would produce an effect like a barrel vault with three facets, two inclined and one horizontal. To construct a flat ceiling in stone was virtually impossible and architects are reasonably practical people. What they did do was to construct two kinds of vault which echoed, as nearly as possible, the visual effect of the traditional structures in timber. One was the continuous barrel vault, the other was a barrel vault divided into bays by transverse ribs which simulated the trusses in a timber roof and gave an appearance of point loads along the wall though, in fact, the load of the vault was continuous. Often there were buttresses on the outside of the wall corresponding to the ribs inside.

37

These buttresses on the wall were sometimes strengthened, often at a later date, by half arches. Thus two great inventions were anticipated without being understood; they were the concentration of loads upon points or piers, rather than walls, and the flying buttress. These were to be important elements of Gothic architecture.

This persistence of old forms in new structures (see p. 15) is an aspect of human nature which appears, in greater or less degree, in the design of all periods and it is reasonable to suppose that it was effective in the Romanesque period.

Our other indication is the nature of the mental processes of architects which even

Vézelay, the nave

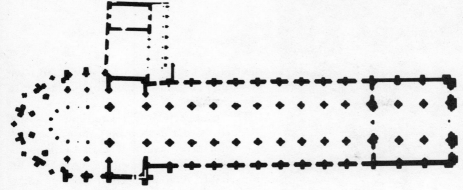

Vézelay, plan. Notice the large narthex at the west end and the full chevet at the east end

in our own time can still be peculiar. Like all designers, architects are susceptible to fashion, and all the more so when they say they are most strongly opposed to it. Out of all the possible ways of building available to the modern architect certain structural forms are accepted and all others are rejected. The most catholic period in all history was the second half of the nineteenth century, when immense variation of style was permissible, but the modern architect is practically incapable of thinking outside the currently fashionable range of shapes. There is thought to be something very peculiar about a modern architectural student who uses arches in his designs. Such an aberration is quickly suppressed! It is arguable (indeed it is probably true) that modern preferences for structural

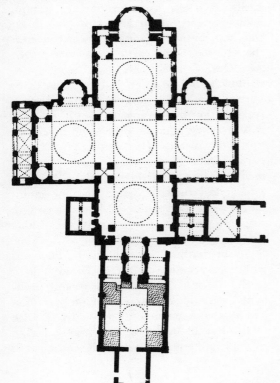

Above Angoulême Cathedral, interior. A basilican church roofed with domes carried on pendentives

Left Périgueux, St Front, plan. This is very similar to the plan of St Mark in Venice

Loches, interior showing domes and horse-shoe arches.
(This is between Tours and Poitiers where the
Moslem army was defeated)

shapes are rationally based upon structural,
functional and economic considerations but
this is not the whole of the story. Architects
create a strait-jacket of "vocabulary" and if
we look back over history we must conclude
that this too is a permanent quality of human
nature as expressed in architecture. It used to
be seen in the creation and persistence of
local styles, but modern transport and communication media have brought us all together under the tyranny of a world style.

Taking into account what has been said
above, we may suppose that Romanesque
architects were capable of thinking and
designing within certain limits but that their
minds were closed, as are those of most
modern architects, to solutions outside those
limits. This may help to explain the persistence of the barrel vault, which was a primitive
form of construction and presented the ghastly
risk that any slipping of either wall would
crack it from end to end and let it fall down
into the nave, which in not a few cases
it did. A strong influence must also have been

the fact that there was a barrel-vaulted nave
at Cluny, the most important monastery in
France.

The transverse barrel vaults at Tournus
(they replaced a timber roof) must have been
the work of a genius, a man of immense
originality, and there seems to have been an
improbably high proportion of such architectural minds in Romanesque France.

The obvious alternative to the long barrel
vault over the nave was the cross vault which
had been used by the Romans (see p. 11),
and was in general use in Romanesque
churches for covering the aisles. To put such
vaults over the nave meant concentrating
huge thrusts at points along the thin walls
which had become customary in timber
roofed basilicas and the astonishing thing is
that some Romanesque architects accepted
this challenge. The nave at Vézelay in
Burgundy is brilliantly light, like an Italian
basilica. It has transverse arches forming
compartments which are cross-vaulted but
the vaults spring low and there is no triforium,
the aisle roof being partly flat to save height.
At Vézelay half-arches lean against the
shallow wall buttresses, but the true flying
buttress was not conceived until architects
realized that by loading the foot of the arch
with a heavy pinnacle they could divert the
thrust downwards. It appears that Romanesque architects were empirical and experimental rather than theoretical in their ap-
proach to structural design and the multi-
dimensional perception of linear forces in
structure was not to come until the Gothic
period.

To the south of Auvergne, at Le Puy, and
within easy reach of Burgundy, we find a
totally different solution to the roofing problem. The source of it appears to be Byzantine
and it extends across southern-central France
to the Bay of Biscay with its most notable
example of Périgueux, where the church of St

Front has a plan which closely resembles St Mark's in Venice. But Le Puy, in Auvergne, owes its domes and much of its detail design to Moorish influences from Spain. It was on the pilgrimage route to Santiago de Compostela, one of the greatest pilgrimages of the Romanesque period. Here, in central France, we become aware of the interlocking complexities of influence. The Arabs learned architecture from the Byzantines and took it to Spain, whence it flowed back into France to Le Puy, meeting and crossing a wave of Hellenesque influence which came through Venice, Lombardy and Milan. The Romanesque period was characterized by movement of people, partly for political reasons, but most importantly for religious purposes, both on pilgrimages and on journeys about church business. This movement of intelligent people, this social fluidity fostered by a Church which offered facilities to rich and poor, to scholar, politician and prelate, encouraged the dissemination of ideas. Localities developed recognizable schools and sub-schools of design, partly for the reasons we have noticed above, but the influences in any one of these are hard to disentangle. It is fair to say that French Romanesque architecture expresses both the tenacity of local tradition and the flexibility of a much-travelling people. Ideas are like seeds and they flourish where the conditions are favourable for them. The parable of the sower is relevant to architecture and helps us to understand why the exploration of French Romanesque church architecture can present so many surprises.

Domes can be built in several ways. One is to lay rings of stone which may or may not be slightly tilted towards the centre. Each ring slightly overhangs the one below so that the dome is gathered in towards the top and then closed with a single stone. This was the method used in the bee-hive tombs of Mycenae and it has the great advantage that it requires no temporary support with timber "centering" during construction. The masons can work from the outside, standing on the work they have already done which is "locked" every time a circle is completed. Such domes tend to be pointed and to avoid this many domes were built with a combination of the above corbelled construction and a "voussoir" system to close the centre. In other words, the corbelled lower part forms an abutment for the arched centre section. Domes can be built of concrete which sets into a monolithic lid, as in the Pantheon in Rome, or they can be completely voussoir domes which can be thought of as arches turned on their vertical axis. A corbel dome consisting of flat rings of stone exerts little or no lateral thrust, but a voussoir dome depends upon the strength of its abutments or on some other method of keeping it together at the base such as a chain, which was used in many Renaissance domes.

The dome is an obvious shape for roofing a space circular in the plan but round rooms are often inconvenient. In later Roman times, ways of placing a dome over a polygonal and then over a square compartment were invented. If the square plan can be reduced to an octagon, by bridging across the corners, then the octagon can be reduced to a sixteen-sided figure which is so near to a circle that the corners can be smoothed out to make it a circle. In Moorish architecture this method was exploited with great decorative effect, with several stages of transition but the first stage, from square to octagon, is obviously the most difficult. The bridge may be made by using a beam across the corner but timber is unsuitable and stone lintels will serve only for small spans, so arches are used. These are called "squinches." Under such a squinch arch there is a triangular cavity which may be closed in a variety of ways but most usually by a tapering barrel vault or a segment of a dome. It may also be filled by corbelling and in Moorish work such corbels may be carved into curiously beautiful pendent effects.

The other method of making the transition from square to circle requires a much more sophisticated appreciation of structural geometry. It consists in forming a direct transition from the corner of the square to one quarter of the circumference of the base of the dome. This *pendentive*, as it is called, is, in fact a spherical triangle cut from a larger dome. It has the structural properties of a dome so long as it is supported all along its two curving sides from the point at its base. The invention of the pendentive made Sancta Sophia in Constantinople possible. From St Mark at Venice it came to St Front at Périgueux.

Romanesque builders thought naturally in terms of round masonry arches made of wedge-shaped voussoirs and their barrel vaults were built in this way. Hellenesque architects inherited the ancient Greek tradition of the corbel dome and used it extensively, but they were also heirs to the Roman tradition of voussoir domes. They used both and combined the two systems as suited them best in particular cases. It is not always realized by historians that the actual problems of working on the job greatly influenced the way buildings were designed, as they still do. The availability of timber for scaffolding was an important factor, as was the cost of scaffolding and timber centering. Furthermore the main contractors for churches were masons and they had to sub-contract the carpentry work which they would hesitate to do. It is often difficult to determine whether the stones in an existing dome are laid on a horizontal or slightly inclined bed as corbels or whether they radiate from the centre of the span as voussoirs. It is significant that the main concentration of Romanesque domed churches is in western France, with some thirty of them around Périgueux. St Front at Périgueux was built in two stages. The existing west end is part of the old church rebuilt in the late tenth and early eleventh centuries. Its magnificent tower contains some remarkable domical construction which looks as though the influence came from Moorish Spain. The main part of the church is clearly modelled upon St Mark at Venice and dates from the twelfth century. Angoulême Cathedral is a plain hall with apse and transepts. It also dates from the twelfth century and is roofed with domes for which a Cypriot origin has been suggested. It may be reasonable to suppose that domed construction was established under Moorish influence in the tenth century in western France, but later, having become accustomed to domes, the architects improved their technique by learning from the eastern Mediterranean.

One thing is certain: the dome is a very sound structural form and out of seventy-seven domed churches which are known to have been built, sixty still exist. In contrast we have already noticed the relative frailty of the barrel vault.

The final structural development in French Romanesque architecture was the ribbed vault. This was a cross vault in which the ribs were built first as arches across the diagonals of the compartment which was to be roofed. These ribs were then used to support lighter panels or segments and thus the weight of the vault was considerably reduced. But once architects had learned to do this they began to understand the separation of the forces in a structure and to do in stone what had previously been possible only in timber, that is, construct in frame and panel. But the nature of timber was such that it had presented no challenge to the mind. When people started to build ribbed vaults out of small stones, each of which was shaped on the mason's bench and carried up to be placed on the centering, the mason-architect had to

Autun, Cathedral, sculpture by Giselbertus in the
west portal

think very clearly about structure. This was
the real beginning of Gothic architecture.
The pointed arch was quite common in later
Romanesque—at Autun for example—and,
of course, in Moorish architecture.

Some French churches were dark, with
strange effects of light, as in the Auvergne,
and others were well lit, but to the visitor
coming from Italy, all of them must have
seemed austere and rather cheap because he
was used to the bright colours of marble and
mosaic. Here in France they made do with
painted walls and even these were in dull,
earthy colours for none better were available.
The walls and vaults, and even the sculpture
in most Romanesque churches were painted.
A good idea of what they looked like can be
gained at St Austremoine at Issoire where the
decorations have been restored. Many people
find them unpleasant, just as they cannot

conceive of the Parthenon having been painted
in bright primary colours, though there is
certain evidence that it was. It is perhaps
worth recalling that for Saint Thomas
Aquinas, one of the three conditions of
beauty was brightness of colour and there is
much interest in Aldous Huxley's appraisal of
medieval gloom with its "goose-turd greens"
and very little brightness of colour except
for the dawn and sunset, and these were the
colours of heaven. Log fires and candles they
had, and some bright gems which were very
precious, gold and silver, some pigments so
costly, like vermillion and lapis lazuli, that
they were used only for the most precious
illuminated manuscripts. In our age of electric
light it is hard to appreciate the admiration
the people of medieval times had for colour,
even the dull reds and yellows they could dig
from the earth. Even flowers were much less

43

spectacular than they are now.

Colour seems to have been applied to buildings with little sense of relating it to the architectural forms but this is certainly not true of sculpture, which is the special glory of French Romanesque. The relationship between architecture and sculpture is very subtle and it may be recalled that the man in charge of the building of the Parthenon, Phidias, was a sculptor. The close relationship between masonry and sculpture is obvious. In the mason's yard on a big church job, a young man could learn to be a mason, then a sculptor or an architect, or sometimes both. These men lived with stone and thought in terms of stone so it is not surprising that they achieved a very close integration of the arts of sculpture and architecture.

The character of Romanesque sculpture varies from place to place but it has certain general characteristics. The first and most obvious is an intimate understanding of the nature and possibilities of stone as an art medium but there is also an underlying unity of style which seems to derive from classical sculpture; but whereas the Greeks and Romans had generally represented the human form as accurately as they could, the Romanesque sculptors consciously distorted it. They may have been influenced in this by the austere and less representational style of Byzantine art, but they far excelled the Byzantines in the range of their expressiveness and the sheer power of their design which embodies, in appropriate subjects, a deep spiritual quality. They also had the great gift of humour and in working upon buildings which were built to the glory of God they not infrequently thought it appropriate to caricature or ridicule man. They also observed nature and took delight in making fables of stone, with birds and beasts, both real and imaginary.

In classical architecture most of the elements of a building were designed, within the tradition, by the architect. All the columns in a row would be identical and the men who made them had no freedom to vary the design. Only in certain places was any freedom given for the stone-carver to become a sculptor. In Romanesque architecture this was all changed, and though the general form of columns and capitals in a church might be Corinthian every one might be made into an individual and unique work of art. Such freedom might have produced a tasteless diversity but the marvel of these people was that it did not. They had this wonderful sense of form which made the complete integration of the two arts possible, and their work, like that of the Greeks in the fifth century BC, provokes the interesting question, much discussed by the modern architect Le Corbusier, as to whether architecture can ever achieve its highest form without sculpture, either as an integral part, or totally.

We started this chapter in Burgundy, where great monastic establishments (and above all Cluny) provided the opportunities for splendid architectural enterprises. From this region communication with Italy was relatively easy and ideas were interchanged with Lombardy and Rome. The other area which became notably creative in the Romanesque period stretched from Toulouse to Tours, on the Loire, with its centre of gravity around Périgueux in the hinterland of Bordeaux. This was the area of France which had been least affected by barbarian destruction and had retained more of the Gallo-Roman way of life than other parts. It is, perhaps, no accident that these two regions produce the finest wines and the best cooking and have retained their ancient reputation for the creaturely aspects of the art of living. Care for quality of experience is a prerequisite of great architectural achievement.

Two areas remain to be considered –

Tournus, St Philibert, the crypt

'Le Pont d'Avignon'

Souillac, portal sculpture of Isaiah

Provence to the south, and Normandy – very different in character and in climate.

Behind the faded gentility and brash modernism of the Riviera resorts, Provence is still slumberously Roman. The little villa farms are like those in Roman pictures and Virgil would find little to surprise him except the tractor and electric light. One finds ruined temples beside farm buildings which it is easy to believe have been continuously occupied and occasionally patched for a couple of thousand years. We must forget about the dangerous road which winds along the cliffs of Liguria to Genoa because the way to Italy in Romanesque times was by sea and the main port was, as it still is, Marseilles, whence the road led to Aix, to Avignon over the famous bridge, with its fine Romanesque chapel, and up the Rhone valley to Burgundy. Provence was thus a backwater – if one may use such a metaphor for a country which is mostly high and somewhat arid mountains redolent of sweet-scented herbs. The lower Rhone was a formidable barrier and the great country of Languedoc, stretching from Roman Nîmes to Toulouse, is curiously in-sulated from the Mediterranean along much of the coastline by swamps and lagoons. In the valleys which run south and west from the Massif Central the Arian heresy persisted and became focussed upon Albi. Into this southern region influences came from the two great centres of architectural development to the north and though there is much fascinating architecture it is difficult to see this as a notably creative region in Romanesque architecture, though some historians have done so.

Normandy is a very different case indeed. The rapacious Northmen settled down at the beginning of the tenth century and became Christian. Here again we must note that Christianity was the means of civilization and with its acceptance, Normandy, with its vigorous people, was brought into the ambit of international Christian culture. The monks moved in and established monasteries which provided, in medieval society, the welfare and educational facilities, including hospitals, schools, libraries and hotels for travellers. They also taught agriculture, husbandry, corn-milling, gardening, apiary and the breeding of fish in ponds. The building of great

Lessay Abbey, Normandy.
(Reconstructed after war damage)

Lessay Abbey, interior

Poitiers, Nôtre Dame la Grande; the vaults of the chancel with partly original painting

monastic establishments, whose influence permeated almost every aspect of living in this awakening duchy of Normandy, provided great opportunities for architects, who, it must be admitted, practise an art in which success depends, more than in the case of any other art, upon people being able and willing to employ them. Some of the designers and builders must have moved into Normandy from elsewhere. Indeed, it is hard to see how these rude people could have developed spontaneously a high standard in the artistry and craft of building. Yet one astonishing fact is manifest in the buildings themselves in three countries where the Normans built, namely the Sicilies (i.e. Sicily and southern Italy), England and Normandy itself. In all three there is a distinguishing strength and simplicity. Though there are major differences of style between the cathedrals of the Apulian coast and the greatest of all Norman buildings at Durham in the north-east of England, there is also an affinity more evident in architectonic conception than in detail design. Even in detail, however, there is a certain ingenuous cleanness which feels quite different from the smiling comfort of Burgundian design. It must be admitted that such a statement is difficult to justify by objective evidence. Just as it is difficult to explain how one great violinist plays with more understanding than, or a different understanding from, another, so, in architecture, it is necessary to visit the buildings and let them speak.

Due to destruction and replacement, not much of the Norman achievement in Normandy itself has survived but what remains is impressive. It includes one of the most beautifully sited buildings in the world, Mont Saint Michel, which compares with the Acropolis at Athens and Durham in England. Romanesque architects – and their patrons – took a great deal of trouble over the siting of buildings, particularly monasteries.

The keynote of Norman design is simplicity, the working out is austere and massive, the impact is tremendous, like some of the great movements in Handel's music. In Norman church plans the Cluny II version of the basilica was favoured, as at Bernay with three apses at the east end. This form was taken to England. It was also used in the Abbaye-aux-Dames at Caen, one of the two monasteries built by William and Matilda in penance for their marriage within the forbidden degrees of relationship. The capitals of Norman columns depart almost completely from classical precedent and are basically square blocks of stone with lower corners chamfered to join the circular column which is much more solid a piece of masonry than the comparatively slender shaft of a classical column.

With the conquest of England by William in 1066 enormous opportunities were opened there for architects who already had behind them three generations of experience of building in Normandy. The "bright boys" of the time must obviously have crossed the Channel after the Conqueror. Thereafter architecture in Normandy itself tended to move nearer to southern French traditions though it was not unaffected by "feed-back" from England where the really exciting things were happening. Normandy is a pleasant but uninspiring country, perhaps geographically predestined to provinciality, to being a place from which fine people go out to seek fame and fortune. It is a country of wide downlands, cider orchards, cliffs and fishing ports and it retains a quality of austerity which differentiates it from the rest of France. Though we pointed out the difference from Provence, the two regions, south-east and north-west, do have something in common after all. In architectural history, however, Normandy was the nursery of greatness and Provence was a resting place for the past.

4 Romanesque in Spain

The main axis of Romanesque architecture runs from Italy through France to England. Its origins were in Italy but the culmination of achievement came in the Gothic architecture of northern France and southern England. As a result of the Norman conquest French was spoken at the court of medieval England and much of France was under English rule. The great religious orders had important monasteries on both sides of the Channel.

But before we look at English architecture it is desirable to look sideways, to Spain in the west and Germany in the east. The relative importance of their architecture in the Romanesque period is variously assessed with judgements not altogether unclouded by modern considerations. We are here concerned not with recounting the history of Romanesque architecture in all countries but with revealing and contemplating its total achievement. So we shall look at these countries to see what they contributed over and above Italy, France and England. Both Spain and Germany derived a great deal from Italy and France. Both exerted influence upon France and England but not all of this was Romanesque because both were strongly affected by Hellenesque architecture: Germany by its nearness to the East, and Spain

because of its conquest by the Moslems at the beginning of the eighth century.

The Visigoths had settled in south-western Gaul in 414. Making Toulouse their first capital, they extended their dominion into Spain. In 507 they were defeated by the Franks at Poitiers, after which they were confined to Spain with their capital at Toledo. In 587 King Reccared was converted from Arianism to the Catholic faith, to which most of the subject population of Spain already adhered. Yet in spite of this, many factors favoured the continuing influence of the East, not least the fact that the Emperor in Constantinople still held outposts on the south coast of Spain.

Not much survives of Visigothic architecture, if one may rightly give that name to the buildings erected in a country where these barbarians were perhaps less than one in twenty of the population. It is probably unwise to generalise from such scanty remains and it must be assumed that many Roman buildings were adapted and continued in use. One can hardly distinguish a Visigothic style but it does seem that these people looked to the East more than to France. The horse-shoe arch was in use by the seventh century. It differed from the characteristic Moorish arch in being three-centred.

Córdoba, interior of the Great Mosque. Notice the combination of Moslem structural design with Roman-type columns. This is a splendid example of *Hellenesque* architecture

Orviedo, Santa Cristina de Lena

In 711 the Arabs crossed into Spain and quickly conquered all but the strip of northern coast from near Orviedo to the Frankish border. The Christian counter-attack pushed the Moslems back in the eighth and ninth centuries but they remained in control of southern Spain throughout the Romanesque period and established there a standard of civilization unrivalled anywhere in western Europe. Córdoba, with a population of half a million, became second only to Constantinople. The great mosque, now the cathedral, was started on the foundations of a Visigothic church by Abd-al-Rahman I in 785 and finished under his successor Hisham I (788-796). No building in the west at that time was comparable in complexity and splendour.

In the Christian north, architecture flourished in the kingdom of Asturias around Orviedo in the eighth and ninth centuries. Visigothic traditions survived but were modified by influences from Carolingian France.

Generally the Moors were tolerant towards

their Christian subjects but under Mohammad I (852-886) persecution, not altogether unprovoked by the Christians themselves, led to their migration northwards. They took with them Moslem ways of design and built churches, mainly in north-western Spain, in the Moslem manner. Among the best of these is Santa Maria de Lebeña at Santander. The style is called Mozarabic. It was in this period that western civilization collapsed (p. 26). The revival of architecture in Spain came under the direct influence of the monks of Cluny.

French Romanesque arrived as a complete system and the points which must interest us here are the extent of its achievement on Spanish soil and the degree to which Mozarabic and Moorish influence affected it, in Spain and possibly back in France, through masons returning, for example, from Santiago de Compostela to Périgord and Burgundy. As in Italy (p. 15) there has been a tendency for Christian historians to minimise Moslem influence in Spanish Christian architecture but it is difficult to discount it in the dome of the Zamora cathedral and other examples.

San Martin de Fromista, near Palencia, built in 1066, is a simple small basilican church with three apses but the tower and the elevated pseudo-transepts echo, distantly, Auvergne and its low, wide character seems to be indigenous to the peninsula rather than imported from France. About the great pilgrimage cathedral of Santiago de Compostela there can, however, be no doubt at all: it is perhaps the supreme achievement of Burgundian Romanesque architects. According to the *Calixtine Codex* their names were Bernard and Robert, but even here, as Conant observed, there are "cusped and mitred arches which savour of Moorish influence". Work was begun *c*.1075 and substantially completed *c*.1128 but it continued until the eighteenth century. (Externally, the modern appearance is Baroque.)

The fervently independent people of Catalonia, in northeast Spain, were freed from Moslem rule in the ninth century. In the tenth, one of the great glories of Romanesque Christendom began to develop. This is the Abbey of Ripoll. The buildings date from *c*.1020-32 with later additions and a major restoration in the late nineteenth century, but the significance for architecture was not dependent upon the buildings, grand though they are. It was a centre of learning and of contact with Moslem culture, the influence of which is difficult to assess accurately, as such things inevitably are, but it must have been great. Almost certainly the ·mathematician Gerbert of Aurillac worked there from 967. Via Italy and Reims he went to be tutor to the Emperor Otto III and then became, in 997, Pope Sylvester II. The Moslems, as Bertrand Russell has said, were "the immediate inheritors of those parts of the Greek tradition which only the Eastern Empire had kept

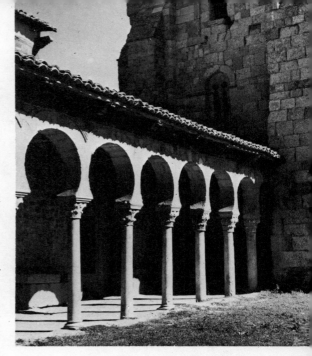

San Miguel de Escalada, near León–classical columns and horse-shoe arches

alive. Contact with the Mohammedans in Spain, and to a lesser extent in Sicily, made the West aware of Aristotle; also of Arabic numerals, algebra and chemistry. It was this contact that began the revival of learning in the eleventh century". One of the principal points of contact was Ripoll.

The use of Arabic numerals was, of course, immensely important for architecture. Consider, for comparison, the problem of multiplying DCLXIII by LXXXVII! The earliest recorded official use of Arabic numerals in the West is on a Sicilian coin of 1134 but they must have been used before this: indeed in *c*.1120 Adelard of Bath, who had disguised himself as a Moslem and studied at the University of Córdoba, published a translation of Alkarismi's *Algebra* (written about 830) under the title *Liber Algoritmi De Numero Indorum*. (The numerals were invented in India *c*. seventh century.) Romanesque architects, like those of most periods, were interested in proportional relationships and they used modular systems based on the sub-

Zamora, San Pedro de la Nave

Zamora Cathedral, the Dome

division of a standard rule. (It was seven feet at Durham cathedral.) They could calculate, as the Romans had done, by the use of an abacus—really a primitive but efficient form of computer—but the value of a compact system of notation in a decimal system of digits such as the Arabs possessed, would obviously be very great. There are some reasons for believing that the pointed arch came from the Arabs but a much more important borrowing was the Arabic numerals, and it is significant that this shortly preceded the development of Gothic architecture with its subtle balancing of stresses. There is, however, no reason to believe that Gothic architects knew how to calculate stresses in the way a modern architect does. The point is that Arabic numerals facilitate numerate thinking.

San Martin de Canigou, interior

Soria, Santo Domingo, sculpture of the portal. Compare with Autun, p. 43

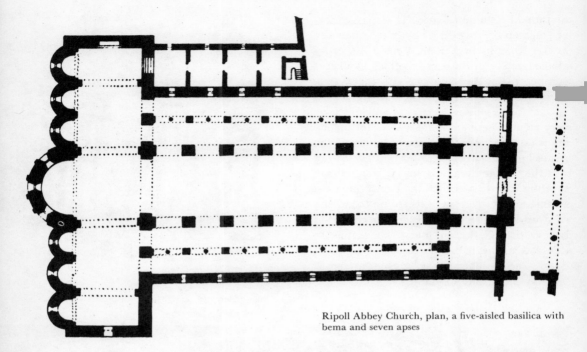

Ripoll Abbey Church, plan, a five-aisled basilica with bema and seven apses

Architects respond to social and cultural forces over which they can exert no control, even if they are aware of them, which frequently they are not. The Romanesque abbey of Ripoll was one of the centres of a new learning which, through the clergy who were the patrons or, in that age, more strictly speaking, the employers of architects, affected all Europe. The fact, however, that architects of the eleventh and twelfth centuries were able to respond with such an outbursting of architectural invention of a high intellectual order suggests that they, as well as the clergy, participated in the intellectual revival. They have left us no records except the buildings, but these, though hard to interpret, are formidable evidence.

The conclusion of this chapter is that though much of Spanish Romanesque architecture derives its direct inspiration from France and from the Arabs, the most important achievement of Spain in the Romanesque period may be, not in forms of plan and shapes of stone, but in stimulating the intellect of architects. We cannot be certain in such matters.

San Nectaire, a typical Auvergne Church

5 Romanesque in Germany

Though territories east of the Rhine had been parts of the Roman Empire, Latin influence beyond the Rhineland diminished with distance. By the fourth century the chief powers in western Germany were the Alemanni and the Franks, pressed in their rear by the Saxons who, by the middle of the fourth century, seem to have established themselves effectively in the north-west of the country. The Burgundians had settled along the Main and the Goths appear to have established supremacy from the Baltic to the Black Sea. In 451 Attila the Hun fell upon the western empire, having already spread devastation in the east. He was forced back from Orleans by the general Aetius, "the last of the Romans", and heavily defeated by the allied forces near Châlons-sur-Marne. Among the allies were the Franks who were, by then, established in north-west France with their capital at Tournai (in modern Belgium), from which Clovis I conquered all of Gaul except Burgundy and Provence.

With the establishment of the Carolingians in the eighth century, the Rhineland enjoyed a period of prosperity and a revival of standards distantly approaching those lost with the collapse of the Roman power. Christianity had come into the region in the eighth century, perhaps mainly from England (p. 63) and the Saxons in the north were partly subdued by Charlemagne. It has been suggested that the consequent curtailment of Saxon sea-power along the German coast opened the way for Danish invasions of England. The existence of a separate nation, in the modern sense, was foreshadowed by the treaty of Verdun in 843. The first half of the tenth century was clouded by civil war and by the invasions of the Magyars, who were eventually defeated near Augsburg by Otto the Great in 955, but during the remainder of the Romanesque period Germany continued to be troubled and divided.

In spite of the turbulent history which has been briefly outlined above, some very fine buildings were designed and erected. The history of this architecture is complex and interesting, with many competing influences, of which the most important came from France, Italy, especially Lombardy, and Constantinople. Furthermore, in the mountain terrain of Bavaria, Austria and Switzerland, which must be included in any consideration of "Germany" at this time, the overwhelming scale of the natural environment had its effect upon the way men built. Another factor must have been the pre-

Issoire, St Austremoine. This is one of the many sculptured capitals in which the basic proportions of the Corinthian order have been maintained but instead of producing a standardized piece of craftsmanship, as Romans would have done, the Romanesque sculptor turned each capital into an expressive and unique work of art

Worms Cathedral

dominance of timber as a constructional material.

In attempting to assess the German achievement in the Romanesque period three salient characteristics are notable. Firstly, the solid chunkiness, the unrefined strength of "German" Romanesque architecture. This has been suggested as an influence upon the Normans. Secondly, the tendency to build tall. There is a strong vertical emphasis, not only in major cathedrals but also in small churches, and this may be a response to the mountain terrain. Towers are composed with majesty and beauty. Even along the Rhine the steep sides of the gorge seem to call for a tall rather than a horizontal expression and in the mountain valleys tall, slender spires stab the constricted space. The third characteristic is a tendency to break up the wall surfaces in rather elaborate ways which may have seemed harmonious with the timber-

framed structure of the domestic and public buildings among which the stone churches were built. In this connexion it must also be remembered that such cathedrals as Worms and Mainz (much altered later) share this somewhat fragmented quality with a great deal of architecture to the east, in Bohemia, Russia and Poland as well as the Balkan States.

The main and most natural contact was with Burgundy, through Alsace, but unlike Burgundy, Germany was not a compact region at the convergence of traffic routes. It was, rather, a vast territory which yielded up its barbarism belatedly to Christian civilizing influences. There is some inclination among historians of architecture to regard Carolingian architecture as essentially German. Aachen, Charlemagne's unofficial capital, is in modern Germany–but we have regarded it as part of the Frankish achievement and linked it more with the development of French Romanesque architecture. Undoubtedly when conditions became more propitious for architecture in the eleventh and twelfth centuries Carolingian influences upon plan and form were effective. On the whole it is not unreasonable to say that there was little *discovery* in German Romanesque architecture. Mainz cathedral in the eleventh century seems to have been essentially a development of architectonic ideas which were inherent in St Martin at Tours as early as the fifth century. Characteristic styles were evolved but there was nothing to compare with the great creativity of the French Romanesque architects. Some of the most beautiful Romanesque of the German-speaking countries can be found in the frontier zone over towards Hellenesque architecture.

The course of history subsequent to the period we are considering has made it seem appropriate to designate national versions of Romanesque in Italy, France, England and to a less extent in Spain. On the other hand, we should be cautious about imposing the German "brand name" upon the architecture of an infinitely complex and vast region which, in the early middle ages, had no conscious unity. Indeed it was very much the contrary. The same could be said of Italy, of course, but there political disunity was less important than a common awareness of Italy's old importance as the heart of the ancient Roman Empire. Germany, on the other hand, seems to have brought forward very little out of its own Roman past. It became instead the heart of the medieval Holy Roman Empire which was to achieve a belated but marvellous expression in German Baroque architecture.

6 Romanesque in England before the Conquest

For Britain "the long sunset" began in the fourth century and darkness began to close in during the fifth, after the Roman forces had withdrawn. Already urban life had been in decline. We may picture a relatively civilized population with an organized way of life, a viable economy and a peaceful disposition experiencing what we can now see as a complete collapse of civilization. The people would not recognize it as such, but they would be worried about "the state of things." Being human they would plan and hope for better times to come. The forces which were to destroy them were inexorable and beyond their control, even beyond their knowledge, for they originated in distant lands and caused the movement of whole peoples who themselves were actuated by the need to survive. Even more mysterious, and perhaps more deadly in the long term, was the growth of inflation, and maladministration of the Roman financial system and the progressive impoverishment of the towns. In Britain this apparently resulted in the growth of a new villa-estate economy which was successful for a while, and curiously anticipated some features of Georgian England.

Despite flickers of prosperity at the end of the third century urban life had begun slowly to decay. British villa estates, being largely self-sufficient, sustained a decent standard of living for a long time. But in the towns, which depended upon providing services, marketing, administration, manufacture and entertainment—all the most vulnerable parts of a civilized society—prosperity declined, houses became empty and remained unrepaired. Investors no doubt complained that "the bottom had dropped out of property" and for architects the outlook must have been bleak indeed. When, at last, conditions improved in the seventh century, England had come into being as a country. Very little survived from Romano-British culture.

The Saxons had been raiding the southeast coast since the third century. The barbarians in the Scottish highlands came back through the old defence-in-depth system which Hadrian had originated but, apparently, the Britons were able to hold them off until the great assault of Teutonic peoples began. Ironically they came first by invitation, to fight for the defence of Britain. With the movement of the Franks into a position where they could control the north coast of France, however, the Saxons, blocked by this new power in the west, crossed the sea in force to conquer Britain. From this time onwards the

Reculver Church, Kent. A small apsidal basilica with
porticus (photo *Aerofilms*)

history of England is one of constant fighting
with two distinct periods of relative stability,
before and after the Danish invasion. This
era closed with the advent of William and the
Norman conquest which brought England into
the axis of the European Romanesque. But the
history of Saxon architecture, prior to this
Norman conquest, is by no means without
interest. It is certainly important as a forma-
tive influence upon the development of
Romanesque architecture on the continent.
A fascinating aspect of Anglo-Saxon architecture as a field of study is that, chaotic though
things were in England during the seventh and
eighth centuries, they were even worse in
most other countries. Consequently, examples
of early Romanesque architecture in England
are quite numerous in comparison with those
found elsewhere. Anglo-Saxon buildings can

thus be the means of insight into the nature of
European Romanesque architecture in its
earliest phases, about which we know so little
from continental sources. As Sir Alfred
Clapham said, England "offered a more
tempting asylum for the dispossessed Greek or
harried Italian than any other available state."
This was especially true after the arrival of
Theodore of Tarsus, an elderly Greek, who
became archbishop of Canterbury in 669.

In England as elsewhere, the progress of
Romanesque architecture was an effect of the
spread and development of Christianity. It
came back to England from two sources, from
Rome through Saint Augustine's mission to
Kent in 597 and from Iona through the
conversion of the Northumbrian king Oswald,
who brought Saint Aidan to establish the
monastery of Lindisfarne, off the Northum-

Hexham Abbey, The Acca Cross, in the south transept

brian coast, in 635. In the history of England, Augustine's establishment at Canterbury was ultimately more important but in the history of Romanesque architecture the Northumbrian Church was much more significant. By a curious coincidence, the greatest monument of Norman Romanesque was to be built at Durham as a shrine of the Northumbrian Saint, Cuthbert, Bishop of Lindisfarne.

The political centre of gravity was in Northumbria and here the great achievements of early Anglian culture were made; Bede's *Historia Ecclesiastica Gentis Anglorum*, Caedmon's poetry, the illuminated Lindisfarne Gospel, the abbeys of Lindisfarne, Tynemouth, Jarrow, Wearmouth, Whitby and Hexham, the splendid crosses with shafts which were decorated with "inhabited vine-scrolls," that is to say, twining plant designs containing animals and figures. This was a decorative

device common enough in ancient Rome, as in the splendid carved pilasters of the Severan basilica at Lepcis Magna, but reinterpreted in the idiom of a new English art. Here we touch upon a matter of difficulty and dispute with which involvement would be inappropriate. It is not irrelevant to our subject but too complicated and contentious on the basis of fragmented evidence to be discussed here. Briefly, the vine-scroll is an eastern Mediterranean form of decoration but both Celtic art in Ireland and Teutonic art from northern Europe embody motifs which may be derived from the same source but have been modified by native genius. Smiths and jewellers in Scandinavia and Ireland were highly skilled in intricate twining decoration. The Book of Kells and the Lindisfarne Gospel are marvels of artistry. The Sutton Hoo burial has yielded objects of great beauty and fine workmanship. The vine is not part of the natural vegetation of north-east England. There is much room for academic dispute and it has been suggested by Clapham that the thesis that the sculpture of the Northumbrian crosses was "an art springing fully armed from the head of a people but recently emerged from a barbaric state," needs careful consideration. It certainly does, but such sudden flowerings have been known elsewhere when opportunity came. It may not be far wrong to suggest that Northumbria was at the confluence of three powerful influences: Celtic Christianity, Anglian vernacular decoration and the direct influence of Greek artists, brought in by Theodore, Archbishop of Canterbury. If the arrival of the Greek masons had been the decisive factor, as some maintain, one would have expected the new art to develop in the south of England but it did not. Admittedly, there were greater opportunities in Northumbria, but the new art was not merely a reproduction of eastern art. It was a reinterpretation and Greeks could hardly have done this alone. Their art

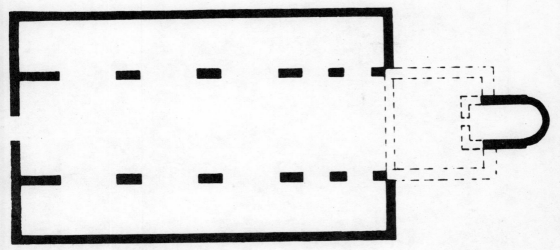

St Wilfrid's Church, Hexham, original plan
(conjectural)

was already decadent. Northumbria probably became a new centre of artistic inspiration because a new, obviously talented people,
uninhibited by tradition, drew inspiration
from several sources. What they achieved was
the re-birth of sculpture, which was to be the
particular glory of Anglo-Saxon architecture.
It antedates the development of sculpture in
Romanesque architecture elsewhere in
Europe by two hundred years.

Early Northumbrian architecture falls into
two groups. One of these we know from
churches like Escomb and Monkwearmouth
which still survive, but these are the smaller
and simpler buildings of the period. Of the
great original churches at Hexham, and Ripon,
we have only the crypts, and of York nothing
remains. These had been built by Saint
Wilfrid, who took the Roman part at the
Synod of Whitby in 663 whereby the ritual of
the Celtic Northumbrian Church was brought
into line with Roman usage. Wilfrid was
several times in Rome and probably built in
the Roman manner. It is known that the
cathedral at York, when it was rebuilt c.770,
had thirty altars. Hexham was a basilican

church with a *bema* and eastern apse. The nave
was a hundred feet long and thirty feet wide.
The total width was about one hundred and
five feet and the total length a hundred and
fifty-five. It was thus a very considerable
building which could have held a congrega-
tion of as many as two thousand people.

A small and very early church is Escomb
in the county of Durham. It consists of a long
narrow nave and a small square-ended sanctuary. The same idea of a long high and narrow
nave with a square-ended sanctuary is found
at Bywell St Peter, in Northumberland, on a
very much larger scale. This church had
porticus on the north and south sides making it
cruciform but these porticus were exedras
rather than transepts. (The word *porticus*
means an exedra alcove or oriel, and is of the
fourth declension in Latin so its plural is
portic*us*, not "portici" as it would be in the
more common second declension.)

The addition of porticus, sometimes to the
extent of surrounding the whole of the nave
and chancel, is a feature of Anglo-Saxon
churches. It seems to indicate a tendency to
design by adding elements (rather than by

Escomb Church, Co Durham

Bywell St Peter; north side. The Anglo-Saxon church extended to the west wall of the present twelfth century tower and possibly beyond

overall conception) which has frequently been a weakness of English architecture.

In southern England, from the time of Saint Augustine, the apse was normally used to terminate the sanctuary of a church. In contrast, and rather curiously, the influence of the austere Cistercian order, in the twelfth century, re-established the square east end as normal in England and gave rise to the splendid east windows of English Gothic

Bywell St Peter; walled-up porticus door in north wall of the chancel. Typical Saxon masonry round the former opening

68

Above Bradford on Avon, interior
Opposite Bradford on Avon, exterior

cathedrals and churches. Compartmentation and rectilinearity are thus foreshadowed in Anglo-Saxon architecture and this provokes thought about the influence of national character traits upon architecture. In modern theoretical thinking function, structural form and the morphology of materials are held to determine the characteristics of style in architecture. Yet they seldom seem to provide entirely satisfactory explanations for the major

69

differences in character which have occurred in the architecture of human communities. Underlying the more obvious and sophisticated reasons for designers working in particular ways there is the evidence of art in primitive societies where tribal design acquires unique characteristics. Subliminally such influences seem to have persisted in civilized architecture but have been very little studied by art historians.

In the use of specifically architectural detail, as opposed to sculpture, Anglo-Saxon architects were remarkably poor imitators of classical features. If there really were as many foreign "experts" as some historians have said came to England, it is interesting to note how

Above Worcester Cathedral, the crypt

Opposite Earls Barton Church, the tower

ineffective they were in getting English workmen to produce classical arches, imposts, capitals, columns and mouldings! This rather indicates that the foreigners were not working masons. Comparisons can be made with the early Renaissance period in England when patrons wanted classical designs but had no means of explaining the precise appearance of what they required. In other words and very shortly, the "experts" were not workmen and neither could they draw. This is not surprising when one realises that the first Englishman who was able to draw architectural details accurately and train English craftsmen to execute them was Inigo Jones in the early seventeenth century. Theodore of Tarsus may have known exactly what he wanted but unlike Inigo Jones he had no means of "putting it over" to others.

Among the characteristic features of Anglo-Saxon architecture is the method of treating corners with quoins called *long and short work* (though there is an example of this in the ruins of Pompeii which should serve as a warning to people who place *too* much faith in stylistic similarities. Pompeii was covered with volcanic ash in AD 79 and remained so until the eighteenth century when excavations were started). Another feature is the arched lintel which occurs at Bywell, six miles away from the Roman station of Chesters, where there are almost identical arched lintels in the baths. The triangular-headed arch is rare but occurs as far apart as Jarrow and Deerhurst. It is not so much a feature of a style as a way of obtaining the effect of an arch without the trouble of building one, but it is an interesting anticipation of the true pointed arch.

Perhaps the most intriguing feature of late Anglo-Saxon architecture is the decorative treatment of such towers as Earls Barton. This has been described as "carpentry in stone," an attempt to reproduce in fire-proof construction the appearance of timber-framed architecture, but it may be derived from the blind arcading of Italian churches, which reached its apogee in Pisa Cathedral. Architectural history provides many such instances, in which a posthumous conversation with the architect might well confound many respectable architectural-historical judgments. Certain knowledge in such matters is not attainable in the absence of reliable techniques of necromancy!

The Danes, who came to England in the ninth century, spread destruction, destroyed the Northumbrian culture and brought little but a desire to better themselves. Perhaps this was laudable in a way. But in reaction against the Danish invasion Alfred the Great became one of the shining lights in the history of the English monarchy. The role of preserving the new English culture passed to Wessex and under Saint Dunstan, Glastonbury Abbey was one of the principal centres. At the end of the century Norwegian raiders came in yet another wave of piratical invasion. In 1042 the last-but-one of the Saxon line came to the throne of England, Edward, called The Confessor because of his ascetic religious life. He had been brought up in Normandy and came to rule a country which, despite the Danes and because they had not brought much that was creative nor completely destroyed the fabric of English society and institutions, was still "English." Edward failed to weld the Saxons and Danes into a single nation. He looked to Normandy for help and brought in Normans to work for him because they were kinsfolk and friends. By disbanding the navy he opened the way for invasion. It need therefore occasion no surprise that late Saxon architecture is difficult to date with certainty to the years just before or after the Conquest.

7 Romanesque in England after the Conquest

William the Conqueror united England under firm government and secured her shores against invasion. The process was painful to the English and their revolts were ruthlessly suppressed. Much of Northumbria, where Romanesque architecture had first flowered in England, was devastated. William began by trying to work through Englishmen but at the end of his reign in 1087 practically every important office of Church and State was held by a foreigner.

The opportunity for architects was enormous. The monastic orders moved into England, replacing the small, unaffiliated monasteries of Anglo-Saxon times. While the king organized the country effectively upon a feudal basis the great Benedictine abbeys became the instrument of developing a new Anglo-Norman culture and spreading the manifold benefits of monasticism throughout the country. Norman bishops vied with each other in building new cathedrals, the symbols of a new age and an emergent nation. Even the sole surviving Saxon bishop at Worcester felt compelled to conform and "destroying the works of his forefathers laboured to heap up stones," as he is reported to have put it. Thus most of the best Anglo-Saxon building disappeared as a matter of policy. (Recent excavations at Winchester have recovered the plan of the tiny Saxon cathedral alongside the great Norman building which replaced it.)

The new men were vigorous and ruthless. They wanted quick results and the early Norman architecture is not notable for finesse, indeed it is powerful and brutally plain. It was almost certainly decorated with paintings, because they could be done quickly and we need not suppose, as Clapham does, that the talent for sculpture had disappeared. Arts flourish according to opportunity. Saxon sculptors probably had to work on plain walling and carry out such decorative carving as ambitious building programmes allowed. When things settled down, sculptural enrichment at last returned and there were men who could do it. What was done at that time has not always earned the admiration of nineteenth and early twentieth century historians, whose attitude to sculpture remained persistently Victorian. It is only in recent years that the development of modern art has opened people's eyes to the great qualities of Romanesque sculpture. Thus the judgments of Clapham and others, and the theories based upon such qualitative judgments, need to be considered with caution.

Normandy was a relatively new state

Above Brinkburn Priory, detail of the north side of nave
aisle and entrance

Opposite Le Mans, the north aisle of the cathedral.
A good example of the clean "intellectual"
quality of Romanesque design in north-eastern France

Malmesbury, sculpture in the south porch

founded by barbarians and it had learned architecture in France from several sources. Some of the invaders came from other parts of France and the clergy (though many of the highest offices went to monks from Norman abbeys) were by no means all Norman. In any case they belonged to orders with wide territorial ramifications, mostly the Benedictine Order of Cluny. Thus, Norman architecture, both in France and England, was, despite its strong and recognisable character, eclectic. It drew upon many sources, upon the whole experience of France and more distantly, upon Germany, Italy and Spain. (There are even horseshoe arches in the north transept at Winchester *c*.1090.)

The typical Norman cathedral has a long nave (fourteen bays at Norwich), a crossing surmounted by a low, square tower, north and south transepts and a chancel. The east end is either triapsidal, like Cluny as it then was, or of the ambulatory type but without the radiating chapels which are necessary for the complete chevet (p. 29). At Norwich there were three eastern chapels and at Lewes there was a full chevet. With the advent of the Cistercians the square-ended ambulatory was used. At St Albans and its associated Binham

Priory in Norfolk, apses in the transepts produced an east end of seven apses *en echelon*. These examples will suffice to indicate the great variety of treatment of the east end of major churches. A similar freedom and inventiveness is found in every other aspect of design but structurally these churches were not adventurous. The naves were generally unvaulted; the structure was massive and impressiveness was achieved rather by the length of the major axis, the long march of cylindrical columns and round arches towards the altar, than by height as in France. Another factor of considerable importance for

Above Cambridge, St Sepulchre, a round church

Opposite Ely Cathedral, detail of arcading. Compare with Pisa, p.20

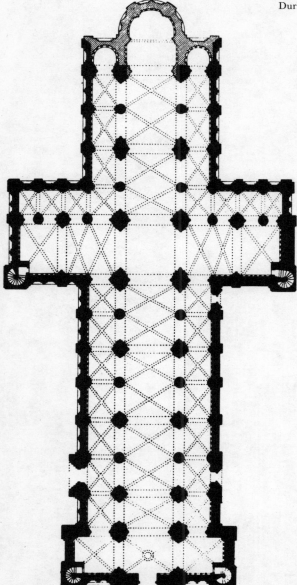

the future, and a contributory reason for the size of Norman cathedrals on the ground, was the fact that Anglo-Saxon towns can have presented few obstacles to "development" as we would now call it. The early sites provided that ample surrounding space which is still so much an enrichment of many cathedral cities.

The climax of the first and most energetic period of Norman architecture in England came with the building of Durham Cathedral, which was started in 1093 with the clear intention of ceiling it completely with ribbed vaults. It was finished in 1133 and was certainly the outstanding structural achievement of the age. Whether this great advance in structural technique was antedated by a few years in France or Italy "there can be no doubt that the cathedral at Durham shows its application in a form easily eclipsing that of its contemporaries" and it was probably fifteen years ahead of anything comparable elsewhere.

What was this great achievement? What was its significance?

For those who have seen Durham Cathedral no explanation is necessary: for those who have not, no explanation is possible. It is one of the great architectural experiences of the world.

The site of Durham Cathedral and the castle which once belonged to the Prince Bishops, but is now the University, is magnificent: a thin, rocky peninsula carved out by the waters of the River Wear at whose mouth is the earlier foundation now known as St Peter's, Monkwearmouth.

According to legend, the devoted followers of Saint Cuthbert were divinely guided to the site of Durham during the anarchy in which ancient Northumbrian civilization perished, but looking at the site today, few could doubt that it was a natural place for a city and the capital of Northumbria. This it remained until the growth of trade, mining and industry made Newcastle more important. But loss of status is often a blessing in disguise and Durham Castle and Cathedral remain substantially as they were in the middle ages. They may well be the finest medieval survival in Europe.

The cathedral was designed to be vaulted so it was made immensely strong. If one goes to Durham looking for structural finesse one may be challenged to think again about the relevance of structural economy to fine design. If we believe that good architecture is rooted in social beneficence we have to admit that this place was the military as well as the religious stronghold of Prince Bishops who wielded almost unfettered power. Looking at it today, when most of the castle provides accommodation for students, we must agree that here is an environment which no modern building can rival on its own terms, even if the heating and plumbing leave something to be desired.

Durham Cathedral is like the Parthenon, and still more like the "Temple of Neptune" at Paestum in being a single unified conception. The additions – the Galilee in late Romanesque style, the transverse chapel of the nine altars which replaced the original apses in the thirteenth century, the effective upward extension of the central tower in the fifteenth century – none of these diminish, but only serve to embellish a powerful single idea. This was the aisled cruciform basilica with apses at the end of the main and each of the side aisles. There were other churches like this but it is a curious fact about architectural design that the roof is the dominant factor. Accept short spans and flat roofs and one gets a relatively undisciplined, flabby design all too easily. Take on the other hand a major structural system of roofing, whether it be the trusses of a medieval timber barn or the lamella roof of an enclosed stadium, or, as at Durham in the last decade of the eleventh century, a new system of ribbed vaulting, and the discipline imposed is like that of the sonnet form in poetry or the sonata in music. The greatest art seems to come from the acceptance and mastery of a discipline, not from the rejection of order.

Durham Cathedral is above all a disciplined design. Its simplicity is overwhelming.

What of the vaults? They were the great innovation. By separating the panel from the diagonal support a whole new field of architectural endeavour was opened up. For the

first time it was understood that it is possible to build in stone, a framed building, like a timber structure but one infinitely more majestic, and, moreover, fireproof. The old groined vaults had been basically the intersection of two barrel vaults, like the intersection of two tunnels in a mine, creating a form which was somehow self-supporting. With the invention of ribbed vaults it was at last understood that the diagonals of the vault could be considered and designed *as arches*. The rest of the vault then became no more than panels of infilling. From this moment, the idea of the frame and the wall were separated and they remained so until the Renaissance. This was the true beginning, the break-through to Gothic architecture.

The curious thing about Durham is that the

Above Romsey Abbey, south transept. This illustrates the formal qualities of Norman architecture at its best

Opposite Durham Cathedral, interior

"way-out" adventurous idea of roofing a whole cathedral with ribbed vaults led to the construction of a super-safe and conservative substructure! Durham is immensely strong and, though some of the vaults collapsed due to faulty workmanship, there has never been any need to strengthen the piers, arches and walls, which still carry some original and some repaired vaults. The building is thus both *avant-garde* and reactionary, in that by the standards of the eleventh century its roof structure is fantastically risky, and the rest is "dead safe". The result, by common consent, is marvellous. For the other extreme of architectural experience one goes to Beauvais or into the choir at Gloucester Cathedral.

Durham Cathedral was designed about thirty years after the Conquest in the reign of William Rufus. It was second-generation Anglo-Norman architecture and though the aristocracy remained for centuries exclusive the number of conquering immigrants had been small. Gradually they were assimilated until a new nation, which was later to wage long and bitter wars with France, came into being. In architecture this new society is reflected by a revival of interest in detail, in decoration and in pure sculpture. Norman architecture, in its last years, before it disappeared into the Gothic which stemmed from the invention of the ribbed vault and the introduction of the pointed arch, became more tender and decorative with ring upon ring of fine carving round the arches of doorways and panels of expressive sculpture.

About 1157, Bishop Hugh de Puisset built the five-aisled Galilee Chapel at the west end of Durham Cathedral. In conception it was unique, in execution it was almost as delicate as good early Gothic work of the period called Early English, but the arches were rounded and heavily ornamented in an old-fashioned, Norman way. By this time, in France, the first masterpieces of true Gothic architecture were being built, among them Nôtre Dame in Paris, and Laon and Noyon cathedrals. The excitement and challenge produced by the Conquest had passed and the progressive movements in architecture were back in France, around the fringe of the old Duchy of Normandy, where numerous Gothic cathedrals were to come into being.

Southwell Minster, the nave.

Opposite Durham Cathedral

Titchwell, St Mary the Virgin; a
small parish church, dating from the
eleventh century, with a characteristic
East Anglian round tower built of
local flints

Laon Cathedral (France). The development of Gothic
architecture out of Romanesque

8 Secular Architecture in the Romanesque Period

So far nothing has been said about secular architecture. The reason is that the development of Romanesque architecture, from the fall of the Roman Empire to the end of the twelfth century, took place in Christian church architecture. People lived in houses, and powerful men built castles to protect themselves and their wealth, but there was no progress in domestic architecture to match the spectacular inventions in building for the Church. Indeed, if we want to study the minor and domestic architecture of the period, the best examples are to be found in the ancillary buildings, the day rooms, dormitories, hospitals and other practical necessities of the monastic establishments.

The fortification of towns was rare in the early Middle Ages, despite the disorder which prevailed. In the sixth century one reads of open towns and shops with goods displayed. If war came it was a disaster which passed over like a thunder storm and life recovered, people licked their wounds, buried their sorrows and carried on. There were villas on country estates, not strong castles nor even peles, those fortified towers within which families could shut themselves away in periods of danger. In the old Roman provinces people continued to live as if the world

were peaceful, while the old order crumbled.

In countries over-run by barbarians some protected dwellings probably existed but the extent of fortification can hardly have been more than a ditch, a bank and a stockade, for this was all the Normans had when they, the strongest military power in Europe, established strong-points in England in the eleventh century. Though we think of the Romanesque period, most of which is comprised within the so-called Dark Ages, as being chaotic, it is of interest to note that the great castle and the fortified walled city belong to the Gothic period though they began in Romanesque times.

Houses must have varied greatly but generally they probably followed the pattern which had existed in the particular locality since Roman days. Often the material, even of big country houses, was timber and practically all Anglo-Saxon and German architecture, other than churches, was timber-built. Little or nothing remains except post-holes from which we can laboriously reconstruct the plan forms. Houses were often simple halls, less imposing as architecture than many a fourteenth century barn. In towns there were some stone dwellings, but their main architectural features seem to have been based on local tradition or ecclesiastical precedents. In any case, very few which can be dated and attributed with reasonable certainty survive unaltered.

In the late Romanesque period castles were built of stone and one of the finest is the Tower of London, still existing in substantially its original form. The Crusades brought French and English knights into contact with Saracenic fortifications, from which they learned much, but the great age of castle building and city walls lies outside the period covered by this book.

How did "ordinary people" live? Mostly in very small houses, little more than huts. Even great kings, when they moved around, took their furniture with them. This in itself speaks clearly about the relative poverty of the age, the lack of creature comforts, and the incredible effort, apparently out of all proportion, which went into the building of great churches.

Domestic life was brutally simple. In the unfortified manor houses on feudal estates the lord and his family ate at the same board with the servants, sat on stools and retired, in the better houses, to a solar. Privacy of sleeping was rare. For the privileged, food was coarse but plentiful. The poor ate black bread and, with luck, some cheese, a bit of butter and a few poor vegetables. Beer was drunk in England, rough wine in France, cider in both countries. Cookery was seldom above the barbecue level and scarcity of meat is reflected in the ruthless preservation of the chase. It was still the sport of kings, and jealously guarded at that, to hunt pigs and deer for the pot.

Against this background of thatched cottages, simple manor houses and motte and bailey castles with no greater comfort, the buildings of the Church, and the standard of living which it set, were in astounding contrast. When the Roman Empire decayed and the barbarians moved in, the intelligentsia of the Roman world had found asylum and an effective means of influence in the Church. Through it they preserved civilization and their monument is Romanesque ecclesiastical architecture, the churches for worship and the abbey buildings for living.

In the villages and towns the principal building was usually the parish church. It was bigger and higher than anything else. It stood not only for the spiritual life but also for education, charity, good behaviour; and within it the nobility knelt down with the peasantry and the artisans. Great castles were obvious by their necessary elevation for reasons of defence, but the climax of every village was its church. In Romanesque times this was designed on the same principles as the great abbeys and cathedrals but was much smaller. It usually had a tower, as the greater Anglo-Saxon churches had done.

Fortunately the rebuilding zeal of abbots and bishops did not extend into all the small villages and many Anglo-Saxon churches continued in use. Some were extended and improved, some replaced, but many survive to the present day and England has a wealth of churches which exemplify continuity from the seventh century.

The typical Norman church was not very different, except in scale. The apse at the east end was common but the eastern tower of Saxon times was often replaced by a central tower and transepts became usual in larger churches. The design was generally simple but with rich decoration round entrance doorways and on arcading. The development of the parish church plan in Norman and later times is a large subject, to which several books have been devoted, and it would be inappropriate to discuss it here. What was achieved in Norman England was a fine vernacular tradition of simple and dignified, spacious church architecture which, over the length and breadth of the country, shows inventiveness and variety of architectonic expression.

Normally churches were rectangular or cruciform but an interesting development, probably due to the Crusades, was the revival of the round or "centralised" church plan. The round Church of the Holy Sepulchre at Cambridge is an excellent example.

It requires a considerable effort of historical imagination to visualise life in Norman England but when the process of feudalisation had been completed there was, for the first time since the fall of Roman power, a sense of order. Probably the kings and bishops, and the officers of state, had little knowledge of history but it seems that they had a sense of man's desperate need, after centuries of strife, for peace and firm government. This, on the whole, the Normans provided, and the message of their architecture seems to be, at the monumental level, power in the administration both lay and clerical; at the lower levels, of manor house, church, cottages and simple industrial buildings such as the mill and the smithy, the acceptance of order. It did not last. The nobility quarrelled, the peasants revolted, the Church was divided by factions and the orders diverged upon principles of life and worship; the power of the monarchy was curtailed by Magna Carta (1215); the State and the Church came into headlong collision with the murder of Thomas à Becket at Canterbury in 1170. The powerful and restrained architecture based upon the round arch of the Romans was replaced by a much more sensitive and flexible form of design made possible by ribbed vaulting and the pointed arch. In their turn, Norman churches were pulled down, altered or extended but, by the end of the twelfth century, the principal architectonic problems had been solved in basic ways. The coming Gothic age was to be a reinterpretation, an awakening, an enlargement of experience, a further step in the progress of civilization.

Bibliography

A selected list of books in English about Romanesque
Architecture for further reading.

GENERAL REFERENCE BOOKS

Conant, K.J. *Carolingian and Romanesque Architecture 800–1200*. Pelican History of Art Series, Harmondsworth, Maryland, Mitcham, 1959 (This is the best general work on the subject and contains an extensive bibliography.)

Nebolsine, George *Journey Into Romanesque*. London, 1969; Putnam, New York, 1969 (A valuable gazetteer of Romanesque Architecture.)

THE CONTEXT OF ROMANESQUE ARCHITECTURE

Allsopp, B., and Clark, U. *Architecture of Italy*. Oriel Guides Series, Newcastle upon Tyne, 1964. *Architecture of France*. Oriel Guides Series, Newcastle upon Tyne, 1963. *Architecture of England*. Oriel Guides Series, Newcastle upon Tyne, 1964.

Booton, H.W. *Architecture of Spain*. Oriel Guides Series, Newcastle upon Tyne, 1966 (Oriel Guides distributed in the USA by Dufour Editions. Chester Springs, Pa.)

MORE SPECIALIZED WORKS

Aubert, Marcel *Romanesque Cathedrals and Abbeys of France*. London, 1966

Busch, H., and Lohse, B. *Romanesque Europe*. London and New York, 1960

Clapham, A. W. *English Romanesque Architecture*. (Vol. I Before & Vol. II After the Conquest). Clarendon Press, Oxford, 1934 (Reprinted 1964) *Romanesque Architecture in Western Europe*. Oxford, 1936

Evans, J. *Art in Medieval France 987–1498*. London, 1948

Fisher, E.A. *The Greater Anglo-Saxon Churches*. London, 1962

Focillon, Henri *The Art of the West. Vol. I*. London, 1963

Lethaby, W. R. *Medieval Art*. (Revised by D. Talbot Rice). Edinburgh and New York, 1949

Rahlves, Friedrich *Cathedrals and Monastries of Spain*. London, 1966

Ricci, C. *Romanesque Architecture in Italy*. London and New York, 1925

Taylor, H.M., and J. *Anglo-Saxon Architecture*. Cambridge, 1965

Index

References to illustrations are in italics